Isle of Man Steam Packet in the Second World War

Isle of Man Steam Packet in the Second World War

Matthew Richardson

Pen & Sword
MILITARY
N IMPRINT OF PEN & SWORD BOOKS LTI
YORKSHIRE – PHILADELPHIA

First published in Great Britain in 2024 by
Pen & Sword Military
An imprint of
Pen & Sword Books Ltd
Yorkshire - Philadelphia

Copyright © Matthew Richardson, 2024

ISBN 978 1 39905 1 576

The right of Matthew Richardson to be identified as the Author of this work has been asserted by him in accordance with the Copyright, Designs and Patents Act 1988.

A CIP catalogue record for this book is available from the British Library

All rights reserved. No part of this book may be reproduced or transmitted in any form or by any means, electronic or mechanical including photocopying, recording or by any information storage and retrieval system, without permission from the Publisher in writing.

Typeset in INDIA by IMPEC eSolutions
Printed and bound in the UK by CPI Group (UK) Ltd, Croydon, CR0 4YY

Pen & Sword Books Limited incorporates the imprints of Archaeology, Atlas, Aviation, Battleground, Digital, Discovery, Family History, Fiction, History, Local, Local History, Maritime, Military, Military Classics, Politics, Select, Transport, True Crime, After the Battle, Air World, Claymore Press, Frontline Publishing, Leo Cooper, Remember When, Seaforth Publishing, The Praetorian Press, Wharncliffe Books, Wharncliffe Local History, Wharncliffe Transport, Wharncliffe True Crime and White Owl.

For a complete list of Pen & Sword titles please contact:

PEN & SWORD BOOKS LIMITED
George House, Units 12 & 13, Beevor Street, Off Pontefract Road,
Barnsley, S71 1HN, UK
E-mail: enquiries@pen-and-sword.co.uk
Website: www.pen-and-sword.co.uk

or

PEN AND SWORD BOOKS
1950 Lawrence Rd, Havertown, PA 19083, USA
E-mail: uspen-and-sword@casematepublishers.com
Website: www.penandswordbooks.com

Contents

Acknowledgments		vii
Introduction		ix
Chapter One	The Phoney War 1939-40	1
Chapter Two	The Channel Port Rescues: Dunkirk and Elsewhere	23
Chapter Three	Royal Navy Service	110
Chapter Four	Keeping the Home Fires Burning	129
Chapter Five	Operation Overlord – 1944	149
Chapter Six	Epilogue	172
Notes		190
Bibliography		196
Index		198

Acknowledgments

There are many people for whose help with the preparation of this book I remain deeply grateful. Mike Royden's website charting the history of Isle of Man and Mersey ferries is an invaluable resource and I recommend it wholeheartedly.

In terms of personal recollections I am deeply indebted to the late Eric Cain who shared with me his fascinating personal memories of D-Day aboard the *Ben-My-Chree*. Eric was an exceedingly modest man, who had a marvellous story to tell. I remain indebted to him for sharing his memories with me, and to Sarah Clucas for permission to use the photo herein.

As ever, the staff of the National Library of Wales were immensely helpful, and I must thank in particular Iwan ap Dafydd.

I must also thank those others who provided family papers or photographs, and who allowed me to use material relating to their forebears, in no particular order David Handscombe, Junemary Moyle, Bernard Scarffe, Lynda Cannell, and Harry Martland; Robert Addie allowed me to quote from his grandfather's narrative of Dunkirk, for which I thank him sincerely, and the Corlett family likewise provided material via the good offices of Darren Prior.

Lastly researcher David Kneale deserves special acknowledgement. He was the first to be granted access to, and permission to publish from, the hitherto closed file at IOMPRO on Government House communications regarding the Steam Packet crews at Dunkirk in June 1940. I am also grateful to Isle of Man Public Record Officer Angela Skitt for clarification of the status of these records.

As an author I am acutely aware that it is particularly easy to cause offence by omission, and from the families of those personnel whom I was not able to mention for reasons of space, no slight is intended; I humbly ask their forgiveness.

Matthew Richardson
Douglas
Isle of Man 2023

Introduction

The oldest shipping company in the world which is still in operation, the Isle of Man Steam Packet Company has played a significant role in the two major conflicts of the twentieth century. It made its ships (and their crews) available to the Admiralty in the First World War, and provided the same service in the Second World War. This time they were to be present at two of the most dramatic moments in world history – the evacuation of Dunkirk, and the Normandy landings – as well a host of lesser known incidents.

The Isle of Man Steam Packet Company has rightly been described as the 'Island's Lifeline' in as much as so much vital food and freight is carried by its ships. In the years prior to the Second World War however the company's role was even greater. In those days the Isle of Man still had a thriving tourist industry, and each year the company's fleet of steamers carried hordes of summer visitors from the cities of England, Scotland and Ireland for a welcome holiday in the fresh air and beautiful surroundings of Manxland.

Ironically, the company had just about completed its rebuilding programme to replace those ships lost or worn out in the 1914-1918 conflict, when war came again. The ships ordered in the inter-war period were arguably the finest that the company had ever commissioned. Built during an economic downturn, the constructors of the *Lady of Mann* in particular could employ only their finest craftsmen to work on her, and she had magnificent cabins, dining saloons and sleeping quarters, as well as powerful engines. This time around the directors of the company would again provide the cream of their fleet to the cause of freedom, suffering heavily both in terms of loss of tonnage and loss of life as they did so. It is often stated that in recounting the history of the Second World War, the losses and sacrifice of the Merchant Navy are usually overlooked. Yet without these men, the war could not have been won.

There can hardly be a finer illustration of this point than the role played by the vessels of the Isle of Man Steam Packet Company in that war. The book which you are about to read is the story of those ships, and in particular of the men who crewed them and travelled in them. Wherever possible, these people have been allowed to tell their stories in their own words, often for the first time.

Chapter One

The Phoney War 1939-40

Whereas the outbreak of the First World War had taken many people by surprise, the slide towards war in 1939 had been slow and gradual; certainly since Munich in 1938 there had been little doubt that war between Britain and Hitler's Germany was almost inevitable. In Whitehall, the Admiralty had made careful plans for the eventuality of war, and even before Neville Chamberlain's solemn declaration on 3 September that the nation was once more in arms against Germany, steps were being taken to requisition a substantial part of Britain's merchant fleet.

During the majority of the Second World War, only the *Victoria*, *Rushen Castle* and *Snaefell* continued to serve the people of the Isle of Man in providing a regular sea link with the UK, as most of the other ships in the Steam Packet fleet were used in some capacity by the Admiralty. There is a long tradition in Britain that in time of war, the Royal Navy can supplement its strength by taking up vessels from trade. The Second World War was to prove no exception to this rule, and shortly after the outbreak of war in 1939 some ships of the Isle of Man Steam Packet Company were requisitioned by the navy and became auxiliary warships. Others were chartered as troop transports, but retained their civilian status. It was an important distinction. Harry Kinley was born at Colby, and grew up at Fistard. The son of a master mariner, his sole ambition as a boy had been to become the master of an Isle of Man passenger steamer. He had joined the company in 1936, after having worked his way up to his master's ticket in coastal vessels operating out of Liverpool and Whitehaven. He remembered:

> When the Admiralty took a ship over, it all depended what type of ship it was whether it was refitted. Now, for instance the *Mona's Isle* that I was in when the war broke out, they brought her in and put guns on her, and all sorts of armaments, bombs, shells, guns, machine guns, anti-aircraft guns all that sort of thing and we didn't do so in our passenger boats, we wouldn't dare put a gun on we would become a man of war then and they could bomb us you see but we were a war ship, as long as you had no armaments of course it was just an ordinary ship. They could still bomb you of course...[1]

His former vessel was now crewed predominantly by regular Royal Navy sailors, and was styled HMS *Mona's Isle* to reflect her new role as a guardship in the English Channel, searching ships for contraband heading to Germany. The same task also fell to the *King Orry*, and shortly after the outbreak of war, naval reservists began to come aboard to replace her regular crew. Her captain was now Commander Jeffery Elliott RNR, although relatively little is known about him as he was to be killed in action later in the war whilst commanding a destroyer on North Atlantic convoy escort duties. Born in Auckland, County Durham, he was first appointed a midshipman in 1911, and commissioned as an acting sub-lieutenant in 1914. By the end of the First World War he was noted as:

> A capable conscientious & trustworthy officer [with] zeal and ability a good and careful watchkeeper with good command of men. Hardworking.[2]

He had been awarded the Reserve Decoration in 1925, and promoted to commander in 1933. Among the enlisted men was an 18-year-old from Connah's Quay in North Wales named Joseph Jones. He had joined the Royal Naval Reserve in May 1939, and when the Royal Navy mobilised in August he was ordered to report to Portsmouth Royal Naval barracks. Alongside Joseph were two other Welshmen from Connah's Quay, Ray Hughes and Sam Jones; like him they had joined the RNR in May 1939, as well as a Scot named Jimmy McCallum from Paisley. After having their kit checked at the naval barracks, all four travelled by train up to Liverpool on the day after war was declared. After leaving the train at Lime Street Station, they made their way to Sandon Dock where they found the *King Orry* swarming with dockyard workers, who were repainting her a dull grey colour and erecting scaffolding on her superstructure.

By contrast, the other Steam Packet vessels on trooping duties retained their predominantly Manx civilian crews.

Two days after the outbreak of war, one of them, the *Mona's Queen* was steaming out of Southampton bound for Cherbourg packed with French reservists who had been working in England. Among the Frenchmen on board were several who had previously tramped the streets and roads of the Island selling onions! The *Mona's Queen*, though not as large as her sisters *Ben-My-Chree* and *Lady of Mann* was a more recent addition to the fleet, and incorporated a number of technical improvements. She was luxuriously fitted out, the ladies' lounge for example being panelled out in light sycamore with jade green mouldings and furniture of mahogany. The smoking room was panelled out in olive teak, the first class entrance and stairway from promenade deck were panelled out in French walnut, the first class lounge was panelled in walnut and birch, and the dining saloon was panelled in Burma mahogany. At her launch in 1934, memories of the First World War were still strong; in his speech to the assembled dignitaries the chairman of directors had prayed to God that she would never be needed for any war purpose, but now she and her sister ships would be kept busy as troop transports, ferrying the soldiers of the British Expeditionary Force (BEF) to France, under its commander Field Marshal Lord Gort VC.

Her station, along with the best ships in the Manx fleet, was now to be Southampton. Other ships from different carriers were also present here – the London and North Western Railway, and Southern Railway for example – but as many of the Manx vessels were ultra-modern oil burners they were widely reckoned to be the best (and certainly the fastest) for trooping duties. Whereas the ships from other companies might make two or three trips per week loaded with soldiers, the Manx vessels would be required to make the crossing every night except Saturdays and Sundays. Having loaded up with troops in the afternoon, they would rendezvous in the evening with other vessels at the entrance to Southampton Water, and the boom defence. A single signal flash would tell the commodore for that night's crossing (masters took this duty in turns) to proceed through the defences, the other ships then falling into line behind him. In complete blackout conditions the convoy would then slip out through the quarter mile long channel between the mines of the harbour defences into open water. Steering a zig-zag course set by the commodore, the miniature fleet would then make its way to the designated port, identified only by a code number. After discharging their troops, the ships would then return home independently, escorted by watchful destroyers. Men of the Territorial Army 48th (South Midland) Division crossed to France on 12 January 1940, and one member recorded afterwards that his battery travelled by train to Southampton, where they embarked at about 3pm. Then:

> At about half past four the *Ben My Chree* slipped her moorings and in the fading light of the January afternoon moved slowly down the Solent. After about three quarters of an hour the ship stopped and in the dusk it was possible to distinguish the outline of other ships. Close to us was a battle cruiser which appeared

to be HMS *Renown* but the poor visibility made identification difficult. Some time during the night we left the Solent and after a rather rough crossing, reached Le Havre early next morning.³

Another soldier who crossed on the *Ben-My-Chree* was a member of the 210th Field Company of the Royal Engineers, named Sapper Don Mason. In his memoir he recorded the journey by train from his barracks to join the Territorial 44th (Home Counties) Division in France:

Eventually Southampton came into view, and the train came to a halt on the dockside almost beside the ship that was to convey the company to France. After being assembled on the dockside and paraded for a roll call, we were allowed to file up the gangway to board the vessel, the name of which I noted was the *Ben My Chree*, it was an Isle of Man steamer now requisitioned for military service.

Again there was a struggle with a kit bag and rifle to push through with a seething crowd all looking for a place to sit, but it was impossible as the saloons rapidly filled up and there were no seats available, and there then began a scramble to stake a claim to a position on the deck of the saloons, which resulted in the deck space becoming littered with kit bags. Finally I managed to get a space on the deck of a saloon and dumped my kit to stake my claim, after which I decided to go out on deck to get a breather.

Other troops were still filing aboard though I could not imagine where they intended to kip as the ship appeared to be overcrowded already. We were certainly not travelling First Class or even Second Class as far as I could see. I continued to wander around the deck watching the dockside activity, until in the late afternoon there were signs that the ship would soon be leaving her berth. I stood at the railings as the seamen slipped the hawsers from the dockside bollards, and the ship began to drift slowly away from the quayside, where the previous frantic activity was now somewhat subdued. It was with very mixed emotions, excitement tinged with a little sadness, that I watched the dockside sliding away. For a while my thoughts turned to my parents, particularly my father, but also to my two brothers and my sister, when would I see them again?

I shrugged these thoughts aside and on wandering back to the saloon I found it was absolutely packed, there was certainly no further space available. At first I had some anxious moments wondering where I had left my kit, but I spotted it and gingerly threaded my way among the men sprawled on the deck.

It was chaotic, we really were packed in like sardines. We had been told that we could sleep throughout the voyage unless required for duty. I could not imagine getting much sleep in these conditions, and as for duty, what were we expected to do on board ship? I soon found out as an NCO bawled out, 'Mason, report to the top deck for anti-aircraft duty.' So threading my way out through the maze of men and their kit bags, I climbed up to the top deck to find that the Lewis Gun had been erected on its tripod. The NCO appeared and said, 'Right Mason, you have two hours' duty with the Lewis, then someone will be up to relieve you,' then as he turned to go he said, 'if you see any aircraft make sure they are not ours before you shoot them down,' somewhat sarcastically I thought.

Our ship the *Ben My Chree* steamed out slowly to the Solent waters where it anchored, the was the rendezvous point where a convoy was to be formed. Throughout the evening ships of all sizes arrived until the area around us was a mass of shipping bobbing at their anchors. It was a lovely evening and the sea was relatively calm, and from my position on the top deck beside the Lewis Gun the scene was a serene and wonderful picture. Fussy naval craft circled the convoy and as dusk fell their semaphore lamps could be seen blinking in the gathering gloom. I wondered if we might encounter enemy submarines during the voyage and mentioned this to a group of seamen, but they assured me that the Royal Navy was the guardian of the convoy and that there was nothing to fear. Any submarines lurking in the vicinity of this convoy will be our own, they said.[4]

Shortly afterwards, Mason was relieved of his duty on the top deck and went back down to the saloon where, to his surprise, with his head resting on his kit bag, he drifted off to sleep as the convoy zig-zagged through the night, Cherbourg being its eventual destination. Also among those who crossed to France on the *Mona's Queen* was the future *Manchester Evening News* journalist John Alldridge, who was to become well known later as an author and screenwriter (he wrote two episodes of Coronation Street in the 1960s). Alldridge was at this time part of a team writing material for armed forces newspapers.

The passenger ships of the Steam Packet fleet continued through the winter of 1939–40 on troop transport duties, but the season was to be one of the coldest in living memory. Harry Kinley, now with the *Fenella* remembered:

I came through the first winter of the war alright but there was a big Flu epidemic and there was only Captain Qualtrough and myself left on deck, as officers; it was snowing this particular night when I was on deck and we had three gangways out loading troops, the commanding officer of the troops came up to me and said we can't get up the gangways any more, they are all snowed up. So I went to the captain and said that we would have to stop loading the troops, he said 'Why, whats wrong Harry?' I said the gangways are snowed up they just can't get up the gangways, we have to stop, the men have stopped even trying to get up with their kits and one thing or another, 'Alright, tell the Commanding Officer to do what the hell he wants.' Anyway, we didn't sail that night, I think we sailed the following evening.[5]

For the *King Orry*, her home port was now Dover. Although her conversion for the armed boarding vessel role had been based upon the work which had been done to her in the First World War, some important lessons had been applied. Her main armament now consisted of two quick fire Mk IV 4 inch guns, and one 12 pounder gun, though this latter was of considerable antiquity and of dubious value. The most significant change was that the part of her main armament in the bow had not been mounted directly onto the forecastle as in the previous war. This forward mounted 4 inch gun was now mounted on a raised platform known as the 'bandstand', the supports for which were bolted to reinforced steel plating, which replaced part of the wooden planking on this part of the deck. This meant that the gun was some 7 feet higher that the foredeck, roughly level with the promenade deck. Locating the gun on the bandstand meant that it was now well clear of the sea water which was found regularly to wash over the forecastle in heavy seas during her previous war service. There was another advantage of this revised method of mounting the gun, in that it would also hopefully prevent the vibration from the recoil of the gun from causing the caulking between the deck planking to work loose.

The other 4 inch gun was mounted on the aft end of the promenade deck, as was the 12 pounder. To prevent similar problems with constant immersion in sea water during rough weather, a steel extension was now fitted to the aft end of the promenade deck, which protruded over the poop deck by some 18 feet and which was supported on steel legs. The stern end of the deck extension finished just above the emergency steering position. Here was located the aft 4 inch gun, like its counterpart supported by bolted down steel uprights. The 12 pounder was mounted on the promenade deck, slightly further forward. The only other armaments fitted were two .303 inch Lewis automatic rifles of First World War vintage, positioned either side of the boat deck.

This early period of the conflict was to become known as the 'Phoney War', because after the initial flurry of activity in carrying the BEF to France to meet the German threat, the two armies eyed each other suspiciously in a hesitant stand-off. The British, who were fully prepared to fight the previous war, began assiduously digging trenches, but there was little other military activity in France. As a result, most of the Manx ships were stood down from active troop carrying duties. The *Ben-My-Chree* and the *Lady of Mann* were moved to the Bristol Channel and were berthed at Newport for several weeks prior to Christmas 1940, and the other Manx ships followed in the New Year. However, it is often forgotten that there was no Phoney War at sea. Ship to ship actions took place from the outset of hostilities and the German U-boats sank both the aircraft carrier HMS *Courageous* and the battleship HMS *Royal Oak* in the opening months of the war, so for the crew of HMS *King Orry* it was necessary to be ever vigilant and watchful.

The Strait of Dover was restricted waters and was blocked by minefields from Goodwin Sands to Dunkirk. Passage through the minefields was controlled by the British and French navies, and any foreign merchant ship wishing to pass through had to wait to be inspected. If they did not, they could be fired upon. The *King Orry* spent an average of seven to ten days at a time undertaking patrol work near Goodwin Sands. Occasionally the crew would get shore leave in Dover, Deal or Ramsgate but the work was monotonous, and exposed to potential enemy attack. The weather was also an opponent; on 1 December 1939 a fierce gale was blowing and the ship sought the shelter of Ramsgate breakwater. In the poor visibility and heavy swell her captain did not see the tanker *British Councillor* attempting the same manoeuvre. By the time they sighted each other it was too late to take evasive action and *King Orry* was struck amidships on the port beam, causing considerable damage. She was left with a large hole in her port side, extending from just above the waterline as far up as her shelter deck. Twelve feet of bulwark on the shelter deck had been ripped away; steel supports had been buckled and deck planking damaged. The *King Orry* made it into Ramsgate Harbour for a closer inspection of the damage, and for emergency repairs to take place. This was enough to keep her afloat, but she was ordered to proceed to the West India Dock on the Thames to enable a more comprehensive inspection and repair job to take place. Arriving there twenty-four hours later, she was guided into her berth by tugs. The next day, civilian contractors came on board to assess the work needed. It was concluded that a spell in dry dock was required, and whilst she was out of commission anyway, work would be undertaken to fit degaussing equipment, which would offer protection against the latest magnetic mines being used by the Germans.

For the crew it meant another thing entirely – an unexpected period of shore leave in nearby London, full of nightlife and as yet untroubled by the heavy bombing of the Blitz which was soon to come. Even more good news came just before Christmas when it was announced that one watch would be granted leave for the festive period, whilst the other watch would get leave for New Year. Repair work continued into January of 1940, the damage repair being more complex than had first been anticipated, and the work of the electricians in installing power cables and other equipment for the degaussing system was also adding to the time needed. Whilst she was in dry dock, living conditions for the crew were less than ideal. The toilets on board were not functioning and so the men had to use facilities on the dockside. With the boilers shut down, there was no steam to provide heating so the ship was particularly cold. Although there was plenty for the dockyard maties to do, there was little work for the crew, and this coupled with the harsh living conditions on board led the captain to send the majority of the men on an additional ten days' leave from 19 January. By the time they returned, the final hull plates had been replaced and a team of contractors had finished repainting the ship's bottom with anti-fouling paint. The *King Orry* left dry dock on 29 January.

With the crew now back on board there was plenty to do to bring the ship back up to fighting condition. Decks were cleaned and rust-stained superstructure repainted. On 2 February an oil barge refuelled the vessel and three days later the ship was re-armed – as a necessary precaution any warship entering dry dock has its ammunition unloaded temporarily – and this was loaded into magazines and ready-use lockers. On 6 February sailing orders were received from the Flag Officer Port of London, and the *King Orry* left with the high tide the following morning, heading down the Thames. There was a brief interlude whilst a compass adjuster came on board – having been stationary on dry land for an extended period it was necessary for her to have her compass recalibrated – but with this task completed she made her way back to the Strait of Dover to recommence patrol duties. She anchored for the night off the Shivering Sands buoy, north of Herne Bay, before the next morning relieving the Armed Boarding Vessel *Lormont* as the North Downs guardship at 10 am. On 10 February those of the crew who had been expecting more of the same monotony that they had experienced before Christmas came in for a rude awakening.

Just after 7am the lookouts reported the steamer *Leonardo* making her way towards a restricted zone. *King Orry* hoisted a signal instructing her to stop, but the captain either did not see the flags or chose to ignore them. In order to get the attention of the *Leonardo*'s master a blank 4 inch shell was fired by the *King Orry*, but still the offending merchantman refused to alter course.

Guardships were required to maintain a head of steam at all times in order to be able to move quickly if required; the captain therefore ordered the crew to weigh anchor and give chase. The more powerful *King Orry* quickly overhauled the *Leonardo* and this time two live shells were fired across her bows, throwing up plumes of water immediately in front of her. This proved successful and she slowed down and hove too. The merchant skipper was informed that he was about to enter restricted waters, and that his vessel would be impounded until his manifest and cargo could be inspected by contraband control officers. The following day there was more drama when, early in the morning a mine was spotted off the starboard bow about a mile away. The *King Orry* approached cautiously, with sailors armed with rifles on the boat deck ready to tackle it. They fired several shots and clearly hit it; although the mine was seen to sink it did not explode, and was possibly faulty.

For the remainder of February the *King Orry* alternated periods of duty as either North Downs or South Downs guardship with periods of leave in Dover or Ramsgate. Conditions were cold in the extreme, the winter of 1939-40 being one of the severest for many years, and on occasions in March snow had to be cleared from the decks, following blizzard conditions. On one occasion visibility was so bad that as the lookouts on the two bridge wings could see little more than those fortunate enough to be in the wheelhouse, the captain ordered that they should be brought inside before they succumbed to hypothermia.

With the arrival of spring, this cold war in Europe began to warm up, with Hitler's first targets being Norway and Denmark which were attacked in April 1940. Belatedly the government of Neville Chamberlain attempted to put together an expeditionary force to support Norway, but it was too little, too late. Junior Engineer Thomas Cannell of the *Ben-My-Chree* remembered:

> After being ashore one evening, I came back to the ship to learn from the gang-way watchman that we were to sail at day break for Norway ... Next day, once the ship reached the open water of the English Channel, we were in thick fog. Normally, this would mean proceeding at reduced speed, but apparently we were under orders to maintain full speed, and so the ship went down the Channel and round Land's End with the siren blowing at frequent intervals. We sailed to the Clyde, and in the early afternoon went alongside at Gourock, to oil and take aboard supplies for the next leg of our journey ... The purpose of our urgent journey we never knew. Perhaps the original intention was that we would carry

reinforcements to Narvik. We now know that the British hold on Narvik was tenuous, so perhaps by the time we reached the Clyde, it was too late to reinforce, and evacuation was more likely. Anyway, we took no troops on board. I cannot recall at what time we sailed from the Clyde, but I remember we passed North through the Minches on a beautiful spring evening, on a calm sea. As the *Ben my Chree* passed Cape Wrath on the North western tip of Scotland some time during the night, a radio order was received for the ship to return to Southampton.[6]

Following the German attack on the Scandinavian countries in April 1940, enemy air activity over the English Channel intensified and there were several Luftwaffe attacks on the *King Orry*. On one occasion a German seaplane flew around the ship and was engaged by her gunners. It flew low and fired its machine guns at them, forcing them to take cover, before dropping a parachute mine nearby. The ship stood by to warn other shipping of the presence of the device, until a minesweeper arrived on the scene to dispose of it. A new addition to the crew of the vessel around this time was Sub-Lieutenant Godfrey Hayes, known as 'Skinny'. He was a 20-year-old Merchant Navy officer from Winnipeg, Canada who despite his youth was a highly experienced sailor. He was a graduate of the British Merchant Navy training school RMS *Conway* who had already sailed around the world. He returned to the UK in 1939 and became a member of the

Royal Naval Reserve, and was posted to HMS *King Orry* on 25 April 1940.

He found the ship at Ramsgate, where she was still acting as an armed boarding vessel, her duty station being just north of Dover in the narrowest part of the English Channel. Here she was able to inspect neutral flagged ships which might be attempting to reach German ports. He remembered that she lay at anchor at one end of a swept (i.e. mine-free) channel, with her anchor cable ready to slip in an instant when required. In the event of one of the passing ships appearing suspicious, or not having the correct documentation she would be ordered to stop and a boarding officer from the guard ship would be sent over to check her papers. If the neutral ship failed to stop, the guard ship would slip her anchor and set off in pursuit. Skinny clearly never saw the *King Orry*'s 4 inch gun, mounted forward on her bow, fired in anger, for he also recalled that the gun was of French manufacture, and no ammunition had actually been supplied for it! This sounds suspiciously like an old sailor's yarn spun for a new young officer. Whatever the truth, on 14 May a bomber flying overhead dropped three bombs, all of which missed their target and exploded in the sea nearby. The following day however *King Orry* was prevented from entering Dover harbour until mines dropped in the approaches had been cleared. This took longer than anticipated, and two days later her fuel situation became critical. The oil fired blowers which drove her steam engines went out, and she was only able to reach her refuelling station with the assistance of a tug.

With the renewal of hostilities the Manx troopships were required to hastily return to Southampton. Harry Kinley remembered that the prescribed Admiralty directions were often calculated by inexperienced WRENs, sometimes with unexpectedly humorous results:

We had one character, a master called Wilfred Qualtrough, he was in the First World War and he knew exactly what was happening down there in Southampton in Naval Control; he had no time for Naval Control at all but he knew what was going on, as a Second Officer he was a navigating officer and it was his job when you get the route – you may be going to Calais, or you might be going to different ports [and] you were routed by the Admiralty and you had to keep to those routes and courses, and the second mates were to make these courses out ... After the first winter of the war ... everything was quiet and we were shipped up the Bristol Channel, the *Ben My Chree*, the *Lady of Mann*, the *Fenella* I was in then and the *Mona's Queen* all shipped up from Bristol Channel ports. We were right at the top of the Bristol Channel and all of a sudden things started to change ... It started again the war, good and proper ... And of course we had to get back into Southampton as quick as we could; we all got our marching orders and went to sail with the route we had to take. I had a private cabin up in the shelter deck doing the navigation, it was my job to plot the route, and Alex Clucas was Second Officer and Wilfie Qualtrough was the Master and I was the Second Mate, and I was making out the course right down the Bristol Channel until we came to Lands End and we had to go around the corner, Land's End into the English Channel and be at a certain buoy at a certain time, about 11 o'clock in the morning we had to be there, not a minute before nor a minute behind we had to be there, it took some working out, but as we were going down along the coast of the Bristol Channel according to the directions I had we were to go across the land, overland! I thought that's not right so I took my own courses then down, around and arrived at the right time because you knew the speed of your ship. Eventually the Second Officer came aboard and Captain Qualtrough, he had a high pitched voice. Alex Clucas, he said 'Captain, you had better have a look, Harry's in there doing the route.' 'Oh, how is he getting on Alex?' 'Well he's got a puzzle here sir.' 'Oh, aye what puzzle's that Harry?' 'Well sir, have you got rollers on this ship?' 'What do you mean?' 'Well you have to have wheels or something.' 'why, what's the matter' So I showed him. 'Oh by ... I was in the First World War and I know all about this sort of thing.' I told him, 'I've got the courses down Sir, down and around to the English Channel and to Southampton.' Anyway, to cut a long story short we sailed that night.[7]

Harry Kinley had spent the whole of the first winter of the war in southern England, without any leave. With the arrival of spring, he was sent back to the Island to relieve some crew on home duties, but he was not there long before other events intervened:

> So I was sent home for three weeks on the home run Fleetwood to Douglas [but] I was only there about just over a week and we had to go into dry dock to be de-gaussed, you see they brought out then the magnetic mine and you had to be de-gaused, the ship had to be magnetised so that the attraction to steel would go away, west instead of east, a wonderful idea. We got into Birkenhead to have this done in a dry dock and there was a telegram waiting for me to proceed to Southampton forthwith, I had only been home a few days.[8]

Kinley's orders were now for him to go down to re-join the *Fenella*, but she had already sailed before he arrived, and so he was ordered to join the *Viking* instead. Events were now unfolding with dramatic speed. On 10 May, Hitler's forces had crossed into Belgium and France. Though the British were the only fully mechanised army in Europe, and the French actually had more tanks than the Germans, both were wrong footed by the lightening advance of Hitler's legions. By advancing through the Ardennes, thought to be impassable to armour, the Panzers managed to drive a wedge between the French and British armies.

With the worsening military situation in France now, following the German attack through the Low Countries, on 22 May the *King Orry* had been taken off regular duties and placed on standby in the Small Downs to await further instructions. Rumours circulated among the crew that some special mission awaited them, but for the time being the men occupied their time by fishing over the side using scraps of food from the galley as bait. The bulk of the BEF, along with some French troops, had now retreated to Dunkirk, from where Admiral Bertram Ramsay came up with an audacious plan to save them – Operation Dynamo. This plan is long remembered for the involvement of the 'little ships', the fleet of fishing boats and pleasure craft which set sail for France to assist with the evacuation, but in fact it was the larger passenger ships which would be the unsung and now largely forgotten heroes of this crucial episode in the Second World War. In particular, the ships of the Isle of Man Steam Packet would play a critical part, and the greatest number of troops evacuated by any one ship were to be rescued by the company's steamer *Tynwald*.

Chapter Two

The Channel Port Rescues: Dunkirk and Elsewhere

The year of 1940 is widely regarded as one of the darkest chapters in British history. Following the collapse of France, for the first time since the Norman conquest (or perhaps the Spanish Armada) the country had been in serious danger of invasion. Yet amid the darkness there was a glimmer of light – the 'miracle of Dunkirk' which saved the BEF and kept Britain in the war. The Isle of Man played more than a fair part in this great undertaking, indeed it could be argued that the role undertaken by the Isle of Man Steam Packet Company in rescuing the bulk of the British Army from France was the Island's greatest single contribution to victory in the Second World War.

On 10 May 1940, the Phoney War came to an end. German tanks and infantry rolled into the Low Countries. The Dutch army fought valiantly but was no match for the might of the Wehrmacht; the Netherlands were overrun in a matter of days. *Mona's Queen*, another modern ship commissioned by the Steam Packet Company in the 1930s, was soon to be drawn into the fighting. Launched just five years before the war, she was a sleek and attractive vessel, especially in her white summer livery. She had been as popular with her crews as with the thousands of holiday makers she brought to the Island during the summer seasons. From 10 May until the day that she was to be lost, the *Mona's Queen* was engaged on missions of special danger to Dutch and Belgian ports, along with three other well-known ships. Before many days had passed, this select little fleet had won the title among the naval men in command of the operation as the 'Hell Fire Squad.' The dangerous nature of their work was fully appreciated by the Admiralty, and two or three days before his ship went down her captain, Radcliffe Duggan received the following message from Admiral Ramsay:

> From the Admiral to H.M.T. *Mona's Queen* – I wish to convey to the captain, the officers and the men my deep appreciation of the excellent work which is being done under the most arduous conditions. You have the admiration of all of us, — Commander-in-Chief.[1]

The opening of the Blitzkrieg saw her on a dash to Rotterdam to evacuate units of the Dutch army, but the Netherlands had already capitulated. Instead, they found Rotterdam on fire and when British aeroplanes arrived and destroyed the huge oil tanks and docks, the sea itself burst into flames as the oil gushed out of the harbour. The next evening the infamous Nazi propagandist William Joyce ('Lord Haw Haw') claimed in a radio broadcast that the rescue ships had been sunk. In fact, enveloped in clouds of thick black smoke, the 'Hell Fire Squad' had escaped from these dangerous waters, only to receive orders to proceed at top speed for Ostend.

The French were determined that as far as possible this war would be fought on the soil of Belgium rather than France, and so they and the British left their carefully prepared positions constructed over the winter, and sallied forth to meet the oncoming German threat. Like the Dutch however, the Belgian army was quickly routed, and it became necessary to try to evacuate as many British citizens as possible from Belgium before that country capitulated. Not a sign of life was visible when the *Mona's Queen* crept slowly towards Ostend harbour just after dawn on 15 May. Captain Duggan later reported:

> I decided to go for the harbour, but just as I approached the harbour mouth a red flag was run up ashore and I got the order to stop. A launch came out, and a Belgian officer boarded us and told me that 'Jerry' had been over and had dropped several mines in the harbour. Shortly afterwards a British destroyer came up alongside and we followed her into the harbour.[2]

The ship berthed and was later on filled up with refugees, shipwrecked crews and Allied soldiers. He recalled later:

> in peacetime, if I had told a Board of Trade official how many people we had on board I am afraid the fine would have made somebody bankrupt. Quite a few of our

passengers had been wounded and shot on the roads by the Hun, one little lad, I shall never forget his head was tied up in a dirty and bloody bandage so I took it off and redressed his wounds, he had a piano accordion and I asked him to play for the people, he was the life of the ship after that and played until he went fast asleep.[3]

Duggan continued his account:

And would you believe it, if there wasn't a Manx person among the refugees, an elderly lady named Mrs. Callister who used to live in Douglas, and Mr. Barthelmy, a brother of Mrs. Farrant, the Deemster's wife. When we were ready to cast off it was dead low water, and I asked what water was in the harbour. A naval officer told me about fourteen feet. When I remarked that my ship drew fifteen feet, he smiled, and said there was plenty of soft mud in the harbour. We took a chance, and sure enough we slithered out through the mud.[4]

This incident is described in G.M.S. Stitt's 1943 book, *H.M.S. Wideawake, Destroyer and Preserver*. The book was published as fiction, but it was in fact an actual account of Lieutenant-Commander Stitt's own experiences with HMS *Whitshed*, with just the names changed in order to comply with wartime censorship rules. The destroyer accompanied Duggan's ship to Ostend, and in the book Stitt tells us that on 16 May, his vessel was ordered to the port to evacuate special refugees:

> On arrival off Ostende about an hour later, Rindale found an empty passenger steamer – the *Mona's Queen* – who had been ordered to embark refugees, lying off the entrance.
> 'What are you waiting for?' he shouted.
> 'You!' was the unexpected reply.
> A Belgian pilot climbed on board and berthed *Wideawake* alongside the SS *Prince Leopold* at the Marine Station wharf, while *Mona's Queen* was secured higher up near the swing bridge.

Although Ostend swarmed with refugees, little seem to be done about getting them aboard, and the threat of air attack (against which there was no defence) grew ever greater. The captain decided to take matters into his own hands, and went to the British Consulate.

> On arrival he encountered a distracted and exhausted official. 'All the baggage has been put into *Prince Leopold* by mistake,' he exclaimed, 'and we don't know how to transfer it to *Mona's Queen* who has been berthed on the opposite side of the harbour. There's no labour to be had, nor means of transport.'

'Why on earth did you not let me know before?' said Rindale. 'I'll soon fix that, and berth *Mona's Queen* where I am, alongside *Prince Leopold*. Then you can call for volunteers among the refugees to shift the baggage. My crew will lend a hand.'

He returned to *Wideawake* at once, cast off from *Prince Leopold* and instructed *Mona's Queen* to berth in his place. No tugs however were available, and, as it was low water, *Mona's Queen* soon got into difficulties. By using *Wideawake* as a tug, and with an excellent display of seamanship, Rindale eventually got her into position and berthed himself on the outside.[5]

More delays followed and it transpired that the British ambassador had not yet actually authorised the refugees to embark. The captain managed to locate him, and appraised him of the danger of the situation. The ambassador immediately authorised embarkation.

Now the order had at last been given, British subjects (many of whom could not speak a word of English!) were able to have their passports stamped. They were then directed to the waiting ships where the officers of *Wideawake* scrutinised the passports and generally supervised the embarkation of the passengers in *Mona's Queen* and the destroyer. Altogether about 1600 were embarked.

At last everybody was on board, and at 4.20 *Wideawake* cast off. But *Mona's Queen* experienced difficulty, and Rindale had to tow her clear before she could go ahead. Then, in company they sailed for England. Thanks to an efficient fighter escort of the RAF, they were not attacked by enemy aircraft and reached Dover safely by 8.30pm.[6]

However when the refugees were eventually discharged from the ship, over thirteen hours was spent by the authorities in examining their credentials. About thirty were held on suspicion of being 'Fifth Columnists' (enemy agents who had infiltrated the refugees) and were stripped completely naked when undergoing examination in order to check for concealed weapons. There was a constant fear throughout 1940 of these supposed enemy agents, a paranoia derived from the Spanish Civil War where it was widely believed that the rapid collapse of Republican forces was due to the efforts of Nationalist infiltrators.

The Wehrmacht advance into Belgium however was a ruse. The real German thrust came further south through the Ardennes, densely wooded country that the French believed to be unsuited for armour. The French army, though it was larger than the German equivalent and in many ways was better equipped, was also low in morale and riven with defeatism. It was also beset by poor leadership, and in the face of German Blitzkrieg attacks many French units collapsed. As the Germans rolled up the Channel coast, port after port fell into their hands. *Mona's Queen* was given the perilous mission of transporting demolition squads to Calais, to render the harbour useless to the enemy. Parties of Irish Guards and Welsh Guards were also transported, in order to provide cover for those involved in demolition. Over fourteen hours were spent in loading some 250 tons of TNT and ammonal on board. On the other side of the channel, there were no harbour staff and no crane operators – all had gone. The 'Suicide Squad' as the demolition team was known began to unload the explosives, and every spare man on board also gave a hand; the task was accomplished in three hours. Duggan recalled later:

> We loaded up with troops there, some of them in a sorry state, tattered and torn but still stout hearted. When we were packed full (we took all that were there at the time) we left for Dover, just left the quayside and going out between the piers when three jerry dive bombers attacked the quayside and station, quite a lot of the explosives were blown sky high, some of those on shore ... being killed.[7]

The *Mona's Queen* got away from the harbour without damage, but how many of the demolition party escaped is unknown. The next trip was to Boulogne, in order to evacuate troops who were bottled up in that port. Here the ship lay alongside the quay under darkness while the troops filed on board; among these was RAF Sergeant Jim Heveron, of 57 Squadron, who were based just outside of Amiens. Shortly after the German breakthrough, the squadron was ordered to fly its aircraft to another airfield, and pile up and destroy all non-moveable stores. The ground personnel were then loaded into lorries and driven to the coast, under frequent air attack. On one occasion their lorry was stopped at a road block, and an army captain tried to issue Heveron and his comrades with rifles and ammunition, but their veteran driver ignored him, telling him he had just 'brats' (RAF slang for young recruits) on board, and proceeded to Boulogne. Heveron would later serve with the famous Dambusters. Duggan again remembered that Fifth Columnists and saboteurs were at work here:

> I was standing on the bridge looking across towards the Imperial Hotel, when I saw a man flashing a torch into the heavens and then disappear up the quay. A few minutes later an enemy aeroplane roared in from the sea and power dived on to the spot where the man had stood. He unloaded his bombs on to the hotel and it was soon in ruins. Luckily, he was too late. The British staff who had been there a few hours earlier were all safe on my ship, including the Duke of Gloucester, who had been injured. That was our last trip to Boulogne, for the Germans were at the harbour bridge head as we came away and his tanks were actually in the town. We were the last troopship out of Boulogne, but a destroyer nosed in after we left and actually took survivors of the demolition squad off one side of the harbour while German tanks made their way down the other side.[8]

As dawn broke, French, British, Belgian and Polish soldiers were carried away from Boulogne and to safety by his ship. As they steamed out, three enemy aircraft swooped down on the quay staff and wiped them out with bombs and machine-gun fire. On the afternoon of 26 May, *Mona's Queen* was ordered to Dunkirk, even before the full-scale evacuation of Allied troops had begun; the ship came under fire from German shore batteries when she was some 12 miles off the French coast. Fragments from one shell actually punched a hole clean through the funnel. The ship's master, Radcliffe Duggan, was known as 'the Rajah' for his statesmanlike bearing. After the event he gave an account of this trip to the French coast to a journalist. He recounted how he was given a course, via a certain buoy. On nearing the coast line he discovered a marker, but was suspicious of its position. He moved slowly towards it to investigate, and found it was a decoy:

> I just discovered it in time for I had hardly shouted 'Hard-to-port,' and was steaming away from it when a salvo of shells from the land batteries dropped all around the decoy buoy.

The heavy shell-fire continued, and the bridge and funnel and upper works were riddled with shrapnel. After they had passed out of range of the shells two German fighter planes dived out of the skies on to them, and ten bombs were dropped around the ship, several only 50 or 60 feet away. Duggan went on:

At the same time, one of our Hurricanes suddenly appeared, and with one short burst from his gun sent the first enemy 'plane down into the sea like a gannet. The same British 'plane also accounted for the second Junker, who went dropping away towards the land in flames.[9]

A large portion of the BEF, trapped by the German pincer, together with some French units now began to retreat towards Dunkirk, the last major functioning port in north eastern France. On 26 May a decision was taken by the British war cabinet that the situation was critical, and the BEF must be evacuated. French High Command was still proposing offensives using formations which had either been destroyed already or whose morale had evaporated, but saving what remained of Britain's army now became Gort's priority. Admiral Bertram Ramsay was given the task of planning the withdrawal, which became known as Operation Dynamo.

Ramsay's main problem however was that Dunkirk, formerly France's third port and possessed of no less than seven dock basins, had been subjected to relentless German bombing since 18 May. The town was now a shambles. The oil refinery which stood at the entrance to the main harbour was blazing fiercely, providing a beacon for friend and foe alike. The bulk of Ramsay's evacuation was initially planned to take place from the beaches outside the town, which could only be approached by shallow draught vessels. To facilitate this, trucks were driven out to sea as far as possible, and the roofs planked over by the Royal Engineers to create makeshift jetties. However, soon it was realised that the East Mole (or breakwater) of Dunkirk harbour could be used as an emergency landing stage. It was not intended for mooring, and getting alongside of the Mole was not easy, but the advantage it offered was that large draught vessels could come alongside it, and they could carry thousands rather than hundreds of troops.

As the evacuation continued Admiral Ramsay requisitioned as much civilian shipping as he could, and a number of the Isle of Man Steam Packet Company ships which had been used by the Royal Navy to transport troops to France were now chartered to bring them home. They were still not commandeered, but were effectively hired for the job, along with whatever crews they had on board at the time. This is an important detail, in the light of later events. However, Ramsay had at his immediate disposal the two other ships which had already been taken directly into the Royal Navy. At Dover was HMS *King Orry* which as in the previous conflict, had been requisitioned on the outbreak of war. Built in 1913 by Cammell Lairds of Birkenhead, in the First World War she had been the sole representative of the merchant service at the surrender of the German High Seas Fleet. Now, most of her crew were replaced by Royal Navy personnel, with the exception of her engineering staff who were retained because of their familiarity with the ship's engines. Her senior crew, consisting of her captain, a Royal Naval Reserve commander with some twenty years of service, an executive officer in the form of an RNR lieutenant, and an RNVR lieutenant as boarding officer, had all seen combat in the First World War but for Skinny Hayes, the navigating officer, this would be a new and terrifying experience. So far his duties had hardly been arduous, as the ship only steamed out a distance of 5 miles from her anchorage in Ramsgate. However after only about three weeks of this, new orders were received and Hayes was instructed to find a chart showing the French coast around Dunkirk. The other requisitioned Steam Packet ship, HMS *Mona's Isle,* had performed a similar role acting as an armed boarding vessel in the English Channel, searching ships for contraband intended for Germany. At the outbreak of war, Harry Kinley had been her second mate, and had taken her into the Herculaneum Dock on the River Mersey, where she had been fitted out with guns and ammunition after being handed over to the navy. A few Manx crewmen remained aboard these ships, but did so as naval reservists rather than civilians.

Mona's Isle reached Dunkirk at about 4:00 am on the morning of 27 May, and waited outside the harbour. Apart from fires blazing in the town, there was little sign of activity and the crew wondered what they should do. Eventually they decided to berth within the harbour and await instructions. HMS *Mona's Isle* was thus to become the first ship into Dunkirk at the beginning of the evacuation. Her crew at this time were probably half and half Manx naval reservists who had been part of her crew before the war, and Royal Navy sailors who had been drafted to the ship. One of the latter group, Sub-Lieutenant Denys Thorp, has left us a remarkable account of that first trip into the inferno. Thorp was a RNVR officer, and had joined HMS *Mona's Isle* in September 1939. He wrote later of the ship's arrival in the early hours of the morning:

> The scene in the port was depressing in the extreme, partly owing to the artificial darkness due to the smoke. There was a good deal of bomb damage and debris and the only signs of activity were a number of French labourers picking over the debris to see what they could find. Astern of us was a British destroyer looking very dirty and battle stained. At about 0530 the troops began to arrive and we were told to take as many as we could and take them back to Dover when the ship was full. When they did arrive there seemed to be an endless stream, no wounded but they were dog tired and dirty and looked as though they had been through many ordeals. There were many from many different units, officers and men separated. They came on board in an orderly stream and distributed themselves about the ship. I remember being approached by one young officer who told me that the general would be arriving shortly and would like a bath. I had to break it to him that we had no bath on board. However when he did appear I found a berth for him in the chart room and felt very sorry for him as he was obviously suffering from great strain.[10]

Like *Mona's Isle*, the *King Orry* was warned to sail on the morning of 26 May 1940, but did not leave her position off the Downs until about 21:00 pm that night. The day was spent in travelling to Dover so that her captain could attend a final briefing, and to enable extra stores to come on board. During the afternoon an Admiralty trawler came alongside and delivered piles of life jackets and a huge quantity of fresh bread. Her crew was told only that their mission was a dangerous one, and that once they reached their destination, the naval officer in charge would instruct them as to what to do.

When the *King Orry* reached the port, it had just suffered an air raid and large parts of it were ablaze, casting a pall of thick smoke. Noting the narrowness of the harbour entrance (partially blocked by a blazing destroyer) the captain elected to swing around and bring the *King Orry* in stern first. This would mean that her exit would be easier should she have to leave in a hurry. Seeing the *Mona's Isle* already alongside, the captain decided to berth next to her. Joe Jones was one of the first ashore as he secured her to mooring bollards with ropes, as he did so marvelling that this was actually the first time that he had ever set foot on foreign soil! Only after they arrived and berthed in the harbour, did they receive further instructions. It was not long before large columns of weary troops began to appear, and in spite of the chaos all around they were calm and waited their turn to board in an orderly fashion. As they did so they were each given a piece of bread and some fried fish from the ship's galley, the first hot food that many had eaten in days. For some it brought to mind the Biblical feeding of the 5,000, with a handful of loaves and fish. Wearing life jackets that they were issued as they boarded, soldiers crammed into every nook and cranny. With over 1,300 men on board, and daylight approaching, the captain decided that now it was time to leave. Among the British soldiers who reached the harbour that morning was Private Dick Cobley, of the 2nd/5th Battalion Leicestershire Regiment, who had hitched a ride with some members of the Royal Army Service Corps in a lorry headed to Dunkirk. He remembered:

> Travelling by lorry, mostly at night, we eventually reached the outskirts of Dunkirk. I had never heard of the place previously. I know we passed through Poperinghe and Armentieres – all heavily bombed. Large oil tanks at Dunkirk were ablaze, planes were bombing and there were fires all around. The lorries were put out of action and we went into the town, picking our way through the rubble with telephone lines dangling everywhere. We managed to get into a cellar where we stayed throughout the day. At night we were told to get down to the 'Mole' where we might get a ship. I remember passing a NAAFI store where we were told to help ourselves to cigarettes – everyone smoked in those days and I brought 400 Gold Flake back with me! We managed to get on a ship called the *Mona's Isle* – an Isle of Man ferry. We crowded on and it was standing room only and no life jackets! I remember

a sailor giving me some fried tomatoes which tasted lovely and we set sail from Dunkirk just before dawn.

The ship went along the coast towards Calais, which, unbeknown to the Captain, was already in German hands. Suddenly shells from the shore began to hit the ship and quite a lot found their target. Luckily we were down below – but I don't know if we could have got out. Then the planes came. They strafed the ship with cannon shells. Twenty-two men were killed and dozens wounded. There was nowhere to dodge to as it was so crowded, and when we reached Dover it had taken over ten hours to cross as the shells had damaged the steering. We saw that the ships funnels were riddled with cannon shell holes – a good job they didn't have bombs![11]

Thorp gives us a more detailed description of this air attack on the *Mona's Isle* during her return passage:

Our anti-aircraft armament consisted of one 12 pounder aft and a pair of Lewis guns on each wing of the bridge. I was near the port Lewis gun when the aircraft were identified as enemy and opened fire on them as they peeled off. This was not however effective. Most of the attacking runs were made from the starboard quarter and our view was thus obscured. The Lewis gunner had by this time taken over and I was acting as loader.

The next thing that happened was a violent explosive crack in our immediate vicinity and I found myself lying on the deck together with the Lewis gunner. He said 'Are you all right, sir?' and I said 'Yes – are you?' and he said he thought he was. So I said well, we had better get on with it, so we continued firing at what targets presented themselves. It was apparent that a cannon shell had passed between us and hit a stanchion a couple of feet behind us. The aircraft circled round until their ammunition was exhausted and then flew off towards the coast. To say I was glad to see the last of them is an understatement. Everyone was suffering from shock in a greater or less degree but nobody on the bridge was injured except the quartermaster who pulled a piece of wood from the back of his head and carried on with the job. The 1st Lieutenant and I left the bridge to survey the damage in order to report to the Captain the situation. When I went down I was appalled by the scene and the condition of the ship. With so many men on board, perhaps half of them on the upper and shelter decks, it is not surprising that there were so many casualties. It was estimated that there were about thirty killed outright and sixty more or less seriously injured. Of the ship's company one officer was wounded by shell fragments in the leg, and one rating was killed while standing outside the chart room door. If he had lain down, his life would have been saved.

Four or five ratings were wounded. Petty Officer Pope RNR though badly wounded in the wrist closed some ready use lockers in the 12 pounder enclosure after the 12 pounder crew were knocked out, in the face of heavy machine gun and cannon fire and afterwards received the DSC. The plight of the wounded soldiers was more tragic as after what they had endured in France, they came aboard this ship thankful to be in the Navy's care and bound for home, with the feeling that their troubles were for the moment at an end. I was very upset by this aspect at the time and it took me a long time to forget that no doctor was carried and no sick bay attendant, but their mates came to their help and did what they could for them. The ship was in a sorry state and when the damage was assessed the situation did not look too bright. It was found that the tele-motor pipes were severed and the ship could not be steered as the hand steering gear had been removed when the ship was converted. All the boats were shot up and rendered useless and the wireless aerial had carried away, the Wireless set out of action. Many steam pipes were leaking and steam and hot water were issuing from unexpected places. The Degausing system which was then outboard had been rendered useless. The compasses were intact and the cliffs of Dover could be seen in the distance. A boat compass was taken down to the engine room platform and we proceeded in the direction of Dover steering by adjusting the speed of the screws. We arrived within about four or five miles off

Dover harbour and were able to contact the destroyer HMS *Windsor* which came alongside and her surgeon boarded us together with a Sick Berth Attendant with medical supplies and they immediately set to work on the seriously wounded cases, which we had been patching up as best we could, one grim scene having been enacted in the galley where the cook removed a soldier's leg.[12]

After this incident, a loud hailer which had been shredded by shrapnel hung in the ship's wardroom, as a grim souvenir of Dunkirk. Astonishingly, in the later war years, *Mona's Isle* was also reported to be haunted by the ghost of one of the soldiers killed on board during that crossing, which she made in tandem with the *King Orry*. Some of these soldiers had only been in France a few weeks, having been sent as reinforcements to the infantry, and many more were from base details and rear areas – cooks, clerks and storekeepers. One of these was Sergeant Dennis Cain of Douglas, who had been serving with the RAOC on ammunition supply lines. After four weeks of bombardment day and night he had made it to Dunkirk. He wrote to his uncle of this return journey:

I came home in the *King Orry* and in front of us was the *Mona's Isle*. She got badly knocked about, and there were a lot of men killed and wounded on her … He put a hole in her side about 4 feet and knocked her steering gear away. That was done from the air just outside Dunkirk. When we turned round on the *King Orry* he opened up with a shore battery on us from Calais. They were French 75s he had captured. He hit us a few times and killed and wounded some, but not as many as on the *Mona's Isle*. It was the speed of the *King Orry* and the way she was handled that got us out of it. She was also attacked from the air, but the planes were beaten off by the A.A. Gun on the ship.[13]

As they steamed along the French coast, all eyes were training upwards in the expectation of air attack, and so it was a surprise when shells began to pitch into the water around them, throwing up great spouts of water. German shore batteries had their range now, and one shell landed close to the 12 pounder gun. The crew were lacerated by shrapnel and blown across the deck by the explosion. The captain now commenced a zig-zag course, but German aircraft had joined the attack. The crew of the *King Orry* blazed away with everything at their disposal until, with the White Cliffs in sight, the enemy broke off the attack.

The *King Orry* was well suited to the task in hand. Built for short journeys at fast pace, the ship was zig-zagging as much as her captain dared within the swept channel and making some 23 knots. The German gunners managed to hit her four or five times, which was an achievement in itself given her speed. She suffered eight killed and forty injured before she was out of range of the German guns on the coast. Skinny Hayes on the upper bridge found himself during the height of this bombardment crouching down behind the splinter mats which had been strapped to the rails, before realising that this padding would be completely ineffective if the bridge received a direct hit. Rather embarrassed by his reaction he looked around, only to discover that the other officers on the bridge were doing exactly the same thing!

Dover was a scene of chaos as ships queued to berth, and soldiers who had been disembarked milled around awaiting transport to camps outside the town. Soup kitchens had sprung up to try to feed them before they proceeded on their journey. For those on the *King Orry*, disembarkation was delayed whilst medical teams came on board to attend to the wounded. Stretcher cases and walking wounded came down the gangplanks to waiting ambulances. Finally when the unwounded troops had left, naval artificers came on board to inspect the damage. Shrapnel holes in the promenade and poop decks were not considered serious, as light damage to the superstructure like this would not prevent her from sailing again. More concerning however was the damage to her degaussing cables which had been ripped away around the stern and had been severed on the port side. This would take twenty-four hours to repair by dockyard workers at Dover, before she was ordered back across the Channel.

On 27 May *Mona's Queen* had also been dispatched to Dunkirk to assist. Making her way through the minefields as she approached the French coast, she dodged shells fired by shore batteries. By this time the Manx ship was coming alongside other ships which had been shelled and damaged and were making their way back to England without having even reached the port. First Officer Clucas remembered:

When we were within two and a half miles of Dunkirk we were suddenly attacked and fired on by shore batteries. The first salvo went over our ship, the next one fell a little short, I thought the third would surely get us, so I ordered everyone to take what cover they could and lay down. In the meantime we had altered course to get out of range. The third salvo again fell short but splinters from bursting shells had badly damaged our degaussing line. One shell had penetrated the mainmast then through two ventilators, hit a davit and scattered shrapnel all over the bridge, one piece having gone through a lifebuoy and then bedding itself in bridge timbers. We got out of gun range only to be attacked by two bombers whose aim luckily for us was poor. They in turn were shot down by one of our spitfires, one hitting the water about fifty yards ahead of our ship … the dropping of bombs so near had damaged the steam pipes of the boiler, however the Chief engineer and Second engineer worked like Trojans whilst we were in Dunkirk and made temporary repairs.

In spite of the heavy shelling and bombing we were having a miraculous escape. As we held steadily to our course and crept slowly up through the minefield to Dunkirk we could see there were no harbour signals, no pilots and no guiding buoys. Captain Duggan then called his men to his side and put the position to them.

'What are you prepared to do?' he asked. 'God knows those lads in there need us.'

'We go where you go, captain,' was the ready answer.

'Then we go on.' said Captain Duggan, and every man went quietly back to his post.[14]

With careful navigation the harbour mouth was reached, but here it was found that the way was obstructed by two sunken trawlers. With 20 feet to spare, the *Mona's Queen* was swung around and backed into what was once a quayside. Duggan takes up the story again:

> It was now a shambles. Men had fallen all over the place, and there were craters on that quay which would take a house. But one thing I saw compelled me to smile It was a large notice on what was left of the wall of a warehouse. 'Defense de Fumer' (No Smoking). And the whole town was one great blaze, while sheets of heavy black smoke drifted out over the sea.[15]

Troops came marching up from the beaches and down through the streets and as many as possible were crowded on to the spacious decks of the ship.

> It's a sight I shall never forget as long as I live. They marched through this heavy shelling and machine-gunning without

batting an eye, never mind breaking formation. They were unbelievably wonderful, and many men carrying their wounded comrades.[16]

Duggan continued with a description of the bravery of some of his crew:

[In Dunkirk] the Naval Officer in change said he wished my signal man to send a message to a destroyer. My Radio Officer went up on top of the Wheelhouse and sent the message without thinking of any danger from machine gun bullets etc. A great bit of work ... nor must I forget Boatswain Mr E. Watterson, he took over the steering whilst we were being bombed and shelled. He stood manfully at his task in a wheelhouse which was to a great extent composed of glass, he acted splendidly in getting troops on board at Dunkirk too. Mr Clucas too and Mr Studholm, 3rd officer worked untiringly. We left Dunkirk about ten o'clock that night.[17]

In fact, Edgerton Watterson the bosun was to receive the Distinguished Service Medal for his bravery that day, and Ambler the radio officer received the Distinguished Service Cross. A journalist who interviewed Duggan later reported:

From Dunkirk, where he rescued 6000 troops, he deliberately steamed four miles through a minefield as a lesser risk to his passengers than sailing past enemy batteries which had plastered his ship on the way in. That was the worst half hour in his life. 'The sweat just rolled off me,' he admits. Captain Duggan went on leave after that experience ... He does not tell us so himself, but he won the D.S.C. For his gallantry in rescuing troops and refugees from France in 1940.[18]

First Officer Bob Clucas remembered that when every man it was possible to carry was crammed into the ship, she slipped away from her berth and under the screen of smoke and fire from land and sea, steamed down the coast until she found the channel leading to the open sea and England. This was the last trip made by Captain Duggan on his beloved ship, for he was about to proceed on a well-earned period of leave, and handed over to Captain Archibald 'Jack' Holkham. Members of his crew later paid the highest tributes to Duggan's indomitable spirit, his courage, and, above all, his wonderful consideration for the men serving under him.

During the night, the *Manxman* had also been dispatched from Dover, her Second Officer Robert Addie compiling a narrative of events. He recorded on 28 May:

Received orders to proceed to Dunkirk. Weighed anchor 18.55 and proceeded. Grounded 22.50 on small sandbank in company with three other boats, precarious position in view of the early rising moon and the possibility of enemy bombing planes. The cause of grounding two buoys marked 'lighted' on charts, actually extinguished (cause unknown).

1230 29th refloated. No apparent damage and proceeded to Dunkirk. 0600 arrived off Dunkirk awaiting berth. Whilst there the '*Mona's Queen*' same Co's vessel was blown up by magnetic mine approximately 1000 feet astern of us and sank in four minutes. Two destroyers anchored close by sent two boats off very quickly to the rescue. We had previously passed over the same spot.[19]

On this, her third trip to Dunkirk, on 29 May 1940 *Mona's Queen* was under the command of Captain Jack Holkham, who had joined the company's service in 1920 as a second officer. Holkham, who lived on Devonshire Road in Douglas, became chief officer in 1928, and captain in 1932, and at one time or another had been in charge of all the company's steamers. When the war broke out, he was in command of the *King Orry*. After that ship was requisitioned by the Admiralty, he captained ships carrying troops to Le Havre, Cherbourg, and Brest, and in fact Captain Holkham had the distinction of being commodore of the first convoy, numbering eight ships, which took troops to France. Considering the speed with which the ship went down after she detonated the mine, a series of remarkable and horrific photographs of this incident exist, which it is believed were taken from the destroyer HMS *Vanquisher*. One shows the cloud of steam which was released from the exploding boilers on *Mona's Queen*. Another shows the ship about to go down. A photograph of the survivors reveals the stress and fatigue from what they have been through, clearly visible on their faces. Many of the officers were not young men, and the effect of being suddenly plunged into cold water laced with diesel oil, amid the screams and shouts of the dying, can only be imagined.

The danger of magnetic mines was however well known to the crew – her master had reported counting seventeen floating free in the supposedly safe channel as she approached Dunkirk harbour on her previous trip. It is widely believed that *Mona's Queen*'s degaussing equipment – a system of electric cables running around and underneath the ship, and powered by the ships generators – had failed. Sometimes, when the crew switched generators, it was possible to forget to reconnect the degaussing system. More likely however is that the failure was caused by the damage sustained on the previous run. Tom Corteen, also of the *Manxman*, confirmed many years later that his ship had indeed passed over the same spot just before *Mona's Queen*, and had not detonated the mine.

Whatever the cause, the ship's back was broken and she went down frighteningly fast. It is reported that it took less than five minutes for this to happen. Most of the engine room crew were lost – the only engineer to survive from *Mona's Queen* was Lacey Knowles. The story reported at the time was that Bob Kneale, one of the other engineers, had been on deck and seen the devastation and flames of Dunkirk. He returned to the engine room and told Lacey that he should see the state of the town. Lacey had gone on deck to see for himself when the mine exploded. Consequently, he was the only one of the engine room crew to survive. Of her compliment of fifty-five, some twenty-four were lost that day.

How the *Mona's Queen* set out on her last voyage was described by First Officer Bob Clucas. Captain Holkham and the ship sailed from Dover for Dunkirk at 2.00 am in the morning. As they passed the North Goodwins they passed every conceivable kind of craft afloat: warships of all sizes, drifters, merchantmen, yachts, and even flat-bottomed lake boats formed part of the Great Armada engaged in the withdrawal of the BEF from Flanders shores. They were very soon under air attack and Clucas remembered some years later:

> Our gunners were splendid and drove the Germans off. They circled round and were returning to the attack when out of nowhere appeared a Hurricane and shot both the German bombers down. Four minutes after the attack, the two Germans were accounted for. It looked as if we were safe for the time being but, the next moment, there was a terrific explosion. We had struck a mine. The ship was lifted out of the water and broke in two and the funnel was lifted clean out of her.[20]

He gave a more detailed description of the sinking to a Manx journalist, just after the events occurred:

> As we drew near to Dunkirk, shrapnel was bursting all around us, and some of the men who would normally

have been on deck went below for shelter. A number of ships were hove to waiting to dash in to the harbour, and we had just signalled half speed and I was observing that another Manx boat was ahead of us alongside the quay when there was a heavy muffled explosion. The captain and all the other officers were on the bridge at the time, and we were all thrown into the air. When I recovered, I found myself sitting on the deck looking aft and I saw that our ship had been blown clean in two.

The main mast had gone overboard and the funnel had fallen into the gap between the two parts of the ship. The engines had been blown out of her and the boilers had gone up so the men in the engine and boiler rooms must have been killed instantly. The aft part of the ship was sinking rapidly on an even keel, but the part we were on was holding up a little in the bows but heeling over. Eight out of ten lifeboats were smashed by the explosion, and some of us made for one of the good boats to launch her, but before we could do anything she heeled over suddenly and we had to clamber along her side which was as level as a deck.[21]

By some strange effect of the explosion he found the port lifeboat floating on the starboard side, and shouting to the others to follow him he made for the boat. Seven or eight of them reached her, and they eventually picked up four men out of the water.

It was impossible for any man who had escaped the explosion to sink, for the sea was littered with debris, oil and about a hundred rafts off the ship. We pulled our wireless operator out of some thick oil, and I saw our cook (Harry Craine) pull the Chief Steward (Alf Morgan) through a porthole. We then observed the paymaster (Mr J.R. Gallagher) trying to climb out through an upper deck window, and a young gunner of the crews who manned the machine guns on board (Gunner Osbourne, of Canterbury), dived into the sea and rescued him. He was alive and conscious when we got him into the boat.[22]

Two destroyers came to their aid and picked up three or four survivors out of the water, and all the time shelling was going on and battles were taking place in the air. One of the destroyers was HMS *Intrepid*, and an eyewitness aboard wrote:

There were at least two French destroyers and one British on the bottom, and several masts of ships sticking out of the water. We were slowly steaming up the coastline in 'line ahead' when we started to pass a small ferryboat named *Mona's Queen* and signalled to the crew. She slowly dropped astern of us, whilst we looked ahead at the landing pier, where a white painted ship was backing out. Just then we heard a dull thump and the deck below us shuddered. I was standing on the side of 'B' turret when sweeping my eyes round quickly saw the *Mona's Queen* lift upwards in the middle. Then before our horrified eyes she broke in two and the two halves rolled onto their sides and she was gone. We lowered our motor boat, which was already turned out on the davits, and they picked up eighteen men and the destroyer *Vanquisher* picked up some. We heard later she was destroyed by a mine. Several ships were sunk by magnetic mines.[23]

Eventually all the remaining survivors were taken on board the *Vanquisher*, where Mr Gallagher died. The body was bound up in a White Ensign and he was buried at sea with fitting naval ceremony, during which, the crew had to answer the call to 'Action Stations' to drive off several enemy aircraft. On the return journey to Dover, two torpedoes were fired at the destroyer, but both missed, and the survivors were landed at the port where they were fitted out for their journey home. Clucas concluded:

> Two things which impressed me on our visits to Dunkirk were the amazing coolness and courage under fire of our soldiers, and the obvious superiority of our Hurricane fighters over anything the enemy sends up into the air. The spirit of the airmen and the soldiers is simply marvellous, and given anything like a fair chance these lads will make certain of victory for this country.[24]

There was great sadness felt in the Isle of Man from the loss of familiar vessels, but the sinking of the *Mona's Queen* in particular, given the speed in which she went down and the high death toll as a result, caused terrible shock. Many of the survivors lived with the memories of what had happened on 29 May for the rest of their lives. The Chief Officer Bob Clucas of Douglas carried a particular reminder of the loss of the *Mona's Queen*. Like other survivors he had little time to collect anything and all his personal effects were destroyed, including his Master's Certificate. This was effectively the tool of his trade – without it he could not do his job – so a replacement was issued by the Board of Trade, but it was endorsed with an official stamp to the effect that the original was lost at Dunkirk. Captain Duggan later paid tribute to the men who went down with their ship and to those of the crew who survived:

> They were without doubt the finest crew that ever sailed in any ship. The cream of sailor men were aboard the *Mona's Queen*, and that goes for the engineering staff, too, and everybody else. This work was not like a summer season where you are with men for a few weeks. I have known and lived with these men for 13 months, and there could not possibly be a more willing, efficient and brave lot of fellows in any ship.[25]

Other vessels from the Isle of Man Steam Packet Company carried on the evacuation, even in the knowledge of the loss of close friends aboard the ships which had been sunk. Addie of the *Manxman* recorded stoically the events later that day:

8.40am berthed at Dunkirk. 10.30am let go, proceeded to Dover for orders. Gunfire and bombing by enemy whilst at pier, which was replied to by our destroyers and AA fire. We had approximate [sic] over 2000 troops on board as we had given out all our lifebelts which number over 2000. Nothing to report on passage. Arrive at Dover 16.15, received orders proceed to Folkestone 1735 disembarked troops.[26]

However disaster, as the old saying has it, is often delivered of twins (or even triplets) and this terrible day was about to become even worse. By now all of the chartered vessels of the Steam Packet fleet save *Viking* and *Manx Maid* (which were both undergoing repair) were heavily involved in the evacuation, and at the same time the air attacks were growing in intensity; 29 May 1940 was to become the worst single day in the company's history for lives and tonnage lost. Making her first crossing now was the *Fenella*, one of the firm's newest and best vessels. She was launched at Vickers-Armstrongs in 1936, a few minutes later her 'twin sister' *Tynwald* also took to the water, the double launch being the first event of its kind in the long history of the company. She had been told to bunker before going to Dunkirk, but as there seemed no prospect of getting oil at Dover, and with the officers and crew keen to get underway, the master and chief engineer decided to sail with the bunkers they had on board. *Fenella* arrived off the port at 1.00 pm on 29 May, but because of a bombing raid she was unable to enter the harbour immediately. As soon as possible, she berthed on the East Mole and loaded troops throughout the afternoon, but with over 600 men aboard, including stretcher cases, she came under pitiless air attack, with bombs landing either side of her. Splinters from one bomb hit her promenade deck, releasing hundreds of gallons of fresh water stored in a deck tank and smashing the engine-room ventilating fans. Mr J.F. Garrett, the lamp trimmer of 5, Circular Road, Peel had been mortally wounded as he was heroically operating a machine-gun which had been placed on the ship's top deck. Many other men were injured by the explosion, but the ship was still seaworthy and her master Captain J.W. Cubbon and his crew bravely continued their preparations for leaving the inferno. However another raid came in about 3.00 pm; this time one bomb struck the Mole and blew concrete debris through her hull, sinking her where she lay, and the next exploded between the pier and the hull, destroying the engine room. Captain Cubbon recalled:

> ... the force of the explosion [blew] out the oil cooler from the ship's side ... completely wrecking almost every pipe and pump in the engine room, rendering the engines useless. I inspected the damage in company with the chief and second officers - the ship was listing badly, fortunately inclining towards the jetty, and was rapidly making water. Our examination of the damage proved that the ship was doomed, and the only course open was to disembark all troops and abandon ship. I instructed the O.C. troops to this effect.

As the jetty abreast of the gangways had been blown away, the only method of disembarkation was to climb over the rails on the forecastle head, which, fortunately, was level with the jetty. The enemy was particularly active at this time, and several times his bombing and machine-gunning held up the disembarking of the troops, but owing to the skilful handling of my chief and second officers, all the troops and stretcher cases were safely disembarked.[27]

When the damage was done to the ship's side, the lighting plant was put out of action, but the engineers descended in darkness to the then flooded engine-room and made their way to the boiler-room to see that all fires were shut down, so as to minimise the risk of the boilers exploding. As the troops were being disembarked from the doomed ship, the other anti-aircraft gunner J. Cowell, who was a member of the crew armed with a Lewis gun, kept up a steady fire alongside two army Bren gunners, until all three were ordered to abandon the vessel. After he had checked that no one remained on the *Fenella*, Cubbon joined the others of his men on the *Crested Eagle*, a Thames paddle steamer which was about to depart for Dover. Robert Holmes of Douglas (a part time boxer, known as 'Battling Holmes') was a member of the crew of the *Fenella*, although were it not for misfortune he would not have been there. At the start of the war he had a safe job at home as an electrician converting Cunningham's Holiday Camp into the Royal Navy's HMS *St George* training camp, until he bought a greatcoat from one of the recruits, not realising that it was stolen navy property. He was dismissed from his job as a result, but his father-in-law James Reed got Holmes a job alongside him, as a fireman aboard the *Fenella*. Holmes wrote afterwards:

> We sailed back and forth to Cherbourg, Le Havre, then set sail for Dunkirk. We were attacked by German planes [and] the *Fenella* was hit amidships, Roy Motion was on duty in the engine room at the time and had his leg fractured. We were told to abandon ship, so we all boarded the *Crested Eagle* ... but halfway down the channel we were attacked by a Dornier who dropped two bombs on our stern. I remember being blown up the staircase in a sheet of flame but still had my wits about me, and looked about for father-in-law [but] I could not find him anywhere so I jumped into the water and was picked up by a destroyer's long boat, and taken back to its parent ship. I was landed at Margate hospital where my burns were treated. I spent two nights in Sea Breeze hospital then transferred to Orpington War Emergency Hospital.[28]

Sixth Engineer Roy Motion, who lived in Melbourne Street, Douglas had been injured by an oil cooler door, blown off its hinges by the blast, which caused a compound fracture of the left leg. This would result in several months in hospital, and one leg three quarters of an inch shorter than the other.

Second (Acting Chief) Engineer Mr J. McLachlan also assisted the injured Motion, who, unaided, had mounted the engine-room ladders, to comparative safety, and as Motion was carried off the ship, he was wrapped in Mr R.W.R. Jones' dressing-gown – the only article of clothing Mr Jones had been able to get hold of in addition to the light garments he was wearing, he having come out of the engine-room only a few minutes before the explosion.

Having boarded the *Crested Eagle*, most of the *Fenella*'s stewards immediately went below deck to assist her stewards, and within a few minutes, Mr Jack Corrin, the *Fenella*'s chief steward, re-appeared on the *Crested Eagle*'s deck with a bottle of brandy, and with complete disregard for his own safety, he moved about the wounded soldiers giving each one a drink to ease the pain of their injuries. Having negotiated the tricky business of clearing the many obstructions in his way, the captain of the *Crested Eagle* had his ship headed towards England and safety when a bomb hit her aft, and in a few minutes fire broke out. This misfortune coupled with a mechanical defect which suddenly developed, forced the captain to beach his ship, and while the operation was in progress, a number of the *Fenella*'s survivors assisted in moving the stretcher cases forward. The words of Engineer Jones, of the *Fenella*, describe what followed:

> We felt the *Crested Eagle* run aground, and soon afterwards a German dive bomber swooped down on us and dropped one right amidships. I don't know what hit

me ... I remember standing on deck and the next thing I remember was two soldiers talking to me on the beach and asking me who I was and what ship I had been in. Some hours later, during which time I was unable to walk owing to an injury to my right leg and back, the soldiers told me someone was calling out for men from the *Fenella*. I asked them to give my name, and in a few minutes Duggie Lawson, our electrician, was alongside me. He tried hard to get me on a ship for England, but the chief concern of the rescuers seemed to be for the soldiers. At midnight, however, he arranged with a naval officer that I should be taken off at 5-30 in the morning and he brought me some rugs provided by the Navy to keep me warm during the night. Promptly at 5-30 a naval party arrived and carried me into a flat-bottomed beat which took us to a destroyer, on to which I was hoisted by a derrick. The naval chaps looked after us well, and when the destroyer reached Dover I was lifted ashore by a derrick and lowered right alongside an ambulance which took me to hospital.[29]

Although in the confusion he had forgotten the name or number of the destroyer, he expressed his thanks to her crew, in particularly her commander and her surgeon, for the way they looked after him. When he reached England, Jones' only personal possessions were a pass which he used at the docks at Southampton, a sheet of notepaper bearing his former address (Brookwood Hotel, Douglas), two snapshot photographs and his card of membership of the Onchan Branch of the British Legion, all of which showed signs of immersion in salt water – so much so, in fact, that the imprint of the Legion badge appeared on one of the snapshots.

Jones recounted later that the most embarrassing part of his arrival in England was the difficulty he had in persuading the hospital authorities that he was not a Fifth Columnist!

There was grave paranoia at this time that spies had infiltrated the wounded, and had travelled with them from the Continent at the time of the evacuation. The absence of proof of his identity, which would have satisfied the authorities, resulted in an application having to be made to him employers in Douglas to confirm his identity.

Chief Steward Corrin, who showed such bravery in ministering to the wounded was lost on the *Crested Eagle.* Though he lived in Liverpool, Corrin was a Manxman and was educated at the Castletown Grammar School. He had been in the employ of the Steam Packet Company for ten years. Mr Corrin's brother, Fred, formerly of Kentraugh, Colby, was also lost through his self-sacrifice in giving assistance to the stewards of the *Crested Eagle.* Also killed was Holmes' father-in-law, James Reed, who was aged 60. Reports at the time indicated that his body had been buried at Dunkirk, but after the war the grave could not be located and he is now commemorated on the Tower Hill memorial.

Great bravery was shown by one of the *Fenella*'s greasers, Joe Simpson, who carried Roy Motion off the *Crested Eagle* when it was hit. Also on board with them was *Fenella*'s Third

Engineer James Corlett, whose friend had been killed whilst standing next to him when the bomb struck *Crested Eagle*. Heavily traumatised by this and earlier events that day, Corlett would not return to sea service for the remainder of the war, instead taking a job on the Manx Electric Railway at the Derby Castle. Amazingly he managed to keep hold of his fob watch, which remained in his pocket despite him being sunk twice in the same day, and this artefact now appears on display at the Manx Museum in Douglas. Among the other survivors of the *Fenella* were the Second Mate Westby Kissack, who later in the 1960s became a captain in the Steam Packet Company, before being ordained in the church, and Fourth Engineer R.R. Kermode who had been sleeping in his cabin when the bomb struck *Fenella*. Dressed only in his vest and pants he left the ship to board *Crested Eagle*. When that ship was sunk he made it on to the beach where by extraordinary coincidence he met his brother-in-law who was driving an army ambulance. Most of the *Crested Eagle* survivors spent the night on the beach, before being picked up the next morning by the *Patria*, a Dutch coaster under Admiralty command. Not among them was Tom Helsby from Liverpool, the *Fenella*'s cabin boy who was wounded and instead was picked up by the Germans. He is believed to be the only Steam Packet prisoner of war of the Second World War. A month or so later his parents received a letter from the chief officer of the *Fenella*, J.E. Quirk who told them of the bombing of his ship and of the *Crested Eagle*. He wrote:

> It was just after this, that Tommy came to me & showed me where he had been burned on his face & hands by the explosion of the bomb, but he was soon bandaged up and said he felt alright ... however the fire gained rapidly and Tommy asked me to lower him into the water – he had his lifebelt on and said that though he could not swim he would be able to float until he got out of the water ... by this time there were hundreds of men in the water and boats trying to pick them up. He said he was alright, and I left him, as there were many more injured men who like Tommy asked to be lowered into the water.[30]

Quirk lost sight of him after this, but it transpired that Helsby had reached the beach and had been taken to a French hospital for treatment. Here he remained for about eight days before the Germans arrived and took him to a hospital in Belgium where he remained for about six months. After this, he was transferred to Stalag IXC, before in 1943 he was repatriated due to his injuries. In total sixteen members of the *Fenella*'s crew were killed at Dunkirk, including one of the oldest Merchant Navy casualties of the Second World War, Greaser James Killey who was 74 years of age. The *Fenella* was to remain at her berth until the evacuation was over, the wreck finally being cleared by the Germans after the battle. In later years it was falsely rumoured that she had been re-floated by the Germans, fitted with new engines, then captured by the Russians at the end of the war. This was a result of a mix-up in the numbering system, which the Germans had used to identify the wrecks in the harbour, and it seems fairly certain that the *Fenella* was cut up for scrap and removed piecemeal in the weeks and months following the evacuation.

Late that afternoon, the *King Orry* was ordered to Dunkirk once again. For her, however, this second trip to Dunkirk was to be the last. There was now much more activity in the port as the evacuation was in full swing. As *King Orry* came into the harbour, she passed the still blazing destroyer HMS *Grenade*, which had been hit by a bomb earlier that day. Replacements for the wounded 12 pounder gun crew had been posted to the ship, and the entire compliment was closed up ready for action. It was not to be long in coming; as the ship approached the harbour a bomber flew in low at about masthead height directly over her. The bombs released exploded in the water around, throwing up great mountains of foam and spray. The gun crews blazed away for all that they were worth, but as a second Stuka made its pass, one member of the 12 pounder crew lost his nerve and deserted his post, running off down the promenade deck and out of sight. He was a critical member of the team, as he was the one who was responsible for inserting the fusing key into the shells, which armed them. Without this, they were useless. The gun captain ordered the rest of the crew to get under cover, and the ship continued with her main defensive armament out of action. She slipped between the East and West Moles which protected the harbour entrance, towards her allotted berth on the inside of the eastern Mole. As she did so, she passed numerous wrecks, one of these being the *Fenella* which had been sunk earlier that day. The *King Orry* was making a slight turn to port when more aircraft appeared. One of the ship's officers, navigator Sub-Lieutenant Hayes, continues the story:

> We were viciously bombed by the dreaded stuka dive-bombers of the German airforce. These aircraft emitted a shrill screaming whistle as they came straight down on your head. I later learned that these off putting screams were caused by mechanical sirens fitted to the undercarriage of the Stukas. About four bombers took part in our little drama. At least two bombs fell immediately ahead of the ship and didn't explode; two or three fell just clear of the stern, exploded and put the rudder out of commission. At least two more exploded close enough to the bow to blow small holes in the side of the ship both above and below the waterline. The noise was horrific and we were all petrified and momentarily stunned. The whole attack was over in seconds and we were left drifting helplessly in the harbour which was already cluttered with wrecks showing above the surface of the water.[31]

The ship's telegraphist, Ernest Lane of Leicester, left the wireless room just as it was shattered by the bomb blast, but was slightly wounded by a machine gun bullet in the leg. He was no stranger to this kind of thing, having been sunk twice by enemy action in the First World War. One of the *King Orry*'s engineer officers was her former Steam Packet second engineer, now Sub-Lieutenant Laurence Quine, who was manning a bridge machine gun when the German dive bombers came in, and in his own words 'gave them some stick!' When the bombs landed either side of her, the blast blew him over the side into the water. Despite a lifetime at sea he could not swim, but luckily landed next to an abandoned life raft and was rescued. The fact that the ship was turning as she entered the harbour had probably saved her from a direct hit and enabled her to stay afloat at least. With her rudder jammed to port, her wheel smashed and bridge telegraph destroyed, the vessel was out of control. Despite the fact that Chief Engineer Stanley Cowley in the engine room had realised what was happening, and without orders from the bridge put the engines full astern, she was still drifting towards the Mole. She struck it hard, causing concrete pilings to collapse and ripping out a section of the wooden walkway. There were soldiers waiting on the Mole to board, and when the ship impacted some of these were seen to fall to their deaths in the sea below. Having set the pumps working in the engine room to keep the rising floodwater at bay, Cowley now went up to the bridge to report on the damage to Commander Elliott. Whilst they were discussing whether it would be possible to control the ship, using just engine power alone to counteract the jammed rudder, both noticed that she was now also developing a list to starboard. Hayes gives perhaps undue credit to Elliott when he continues:

Our captain managed to manoeuvre the ship alongside the mole using the engines alone (no rudder ... no steering). There was still a lot of enemy air activity in the area and we were ordered to abandon ship and get ashore. Unfortunately there didn't seem to be much safety in that course of action because we would have to transit a long, open and completely unprotected pier before we could reach any substantial cover. Most of the ship's company did get ashore, to the dock and huddled there hoping the bombers would not come back.[32]

Now urgent discussions took place as to what the extent of the damage was, and a naval officer came on board to assess whether she was still seaworthy. With the evacuation in full swing he was anxious that she should not founder at her berth. If necessary, he asked if she could be beached in the shallows outside the harbour, where at least she could continue to provide support as a gun platform. Shortly afterwards an inspection party went back on board to examine the hull and to try to ascertain if repairs could be made. Her first lieutenant, Jonathan Lee's report of this survives:

We only received one direct hit, on the stern, which blew the rudder off, and we just drifted alongside the Mole. The *Fenella* was alongside the same Mole, only on the outside, the *Grenade* was blazing away furiously and whilst we were drifting both her magazines blew up.

> After drifting alongside we moored up, and the CO and myself carried out an examination of the ship, and found so many holes from the shrapnel that it was considered impossible to do anything, and it was only a question as to whether or not we could get her away from the Mole. We eventually decided that we must make the attempt, because, if the ship sank, she would be certain to turn on her starboard side and thus block the entrance with her funnel and masts. This was all about 8pm.[33]

Gun crews had come back on board and the missing 12 pounder gunner was located, along with the vital fusing key. The crews kept a sharp watch for any further air attack on the ship or the Mole. Damage control teams worked through the remainder of the day. The smaller holes in the ship's sides could be plugged fairly easily but the vessel was still taking on water and the pumps were only just keeping ahead of the ingress. Any drop in steam pressure from the boilers would reduce their effectiveness, and would result in the vessel sinking. A repair party under Quine managed to free up the rudder a little so that it was in a more central position, but the damage to her steering gear was beyond anything that they could fix without assistance from a dockyard. The steering motors were beyond local repair, the bridge wheel had gone and the emergency steering wheels on the poop deck had been destroyed by the bomb blast. *King Orry* had no steering control beyond increasing or decreasing the power to her port and starboard propellers, but at nightfall, with less risk of air attack, the decision was taken to at least try to get her away from the Mole. Lee tells us:

> The tide was low and the ship resting on the bottom, so we had to wait for about two hours. Then when we came to shift her we found the rubbing strake on the port bow was actually resting on the Mole and the Mole was virtually carrying the whole weight of the ship. It took a tremendous effort of the ship's engines to get the rubbing strake clear and about two hours for us to get the ship out of the harbour stern first, just using the stern engines. Our intention was to beach her out of the way, but suddenly she took a heavy list to starboard and sank almost without warning. This was about two o'clock on the morning of May 30th. We all took to the water, my watch stopping at 1.59am.[34]

Skinny Hayes gives us his perspective of these events:

> When all was ready we slipped away from the pier, very gently, and proceeded to go astern slowly out through the narrow entrance ... here we were, in the dark, going astern, with a wounded ship and a shaken crew – it certainly was not easy. The question in everyone's mind was would the captain turn the ship to port up toward the beaches and drive ashore there, as suggested by the embarkation officer, or would he turn to starboard, toward Dover and try for home? As we were slowly

moving out of the harbour, the executive officer and I went around the upper deck and cut loose all the peacetime passenger benches that were in reality small life rafts. They had been lashed down to special fixtures in the deck many years before to prevent movement in rough seas. Our remarkable executive officer had remembered the lashings and decided that now was the time they might be needed in their secondary role ... while we were doing this, we noticed the ship's bow slowly turn to starboard – towards England. The 'old man' was going to go for it! Our joy was short lived however because as she turned slowly, she also started to list heavily to starboard. At that point I decided that she was probably going to capsize, so I sprinted to my cabin which was on the upper deck to try to save some valuables.[35]

As the ship rolled, Hayes was able to walk along the now horizontal side to swim onto a raft, and as he later remarked, although he got wet the most amazing thing was that he didn't even lose his hat. Lieutenant Jonathan Lee remembered that a steward, in a state of shell shock and traumatised by the bombing, was patiently and meticulously sweeping up smashed glasses from the wardroom floor, even as the vessel was going down. Lee vividly remembered the water lapping nearer and nearer the bridge as she began to settle. As it finally engulfed the bridge he dived from the stern. Wreckage entangled the whistle lanyard, and as the *King Orry* disappeared beneath the water she let out a final moan as if it was her death cry. Men from nearby ships attempted to rescue her crew, and Jesse Elton of Poole, the cook of the MV *Bystander* would later receive the Conspicuous Gallantry Medal from the king after diving in and single-handedly rescuing twenty-five men. Assistance was also provided by three trawlers, the *Lord Grey*, *Lord Collingwood* and the *Clythness*, as well as a motor launch from HMS *Excellent* (the Royal Navy gunnery school at Portsmouth). Hayes adds:

> When I entered the water I swam to the nearest float and found three or four others clinging to it. Three of them were from our engine room who were freezing. They had been on watch when the ship started to heel and got out in time. Unfortunately they were clad in only thin cotton pants and a singlet ... the water of the English Channel was cold! We got two of these men on top of the raft where they could hang on more easily.[36]

A motor torpedo boat was nearby, picking up survivors, so Hayes and a comrade swam over to it to get help. He was taken below, given dry clothes and a large glass of spirits which warmed him up as much as the electric heater that he was given. One of the 12 pounder gunners, Joe Jones was a poor swimmer and when it became obvious that the vessel was about to roll over, he took off his duffel coat and ensured that his lifebelt was fully inflated. In order not to become trapped under the sinking giant he climbed over the higher port guard rail. He fell down the ship's side, hitting the wooden belting before going head first into the sea. He immediately discovered that the water was both freezing cold, despite it being late May, and covered in fuel oil. He involuntarily swallowed some of the foul substance, which also burned his eyes and nose. Swimming away as best he could, he became aware behind him of a screech of grinding metal and the hiss of escaping steam, followed by a gurgling sound, then silence. The *King Orry* had gone. Calling out for help, Jones was pulled aboard a life raft which had been cut loose from the deck, by Leading Telegraphist Nugent and Able Seaman Smith, both members of the Royal Fleet Reserve. Shivering uncontrollably now, he waited what seemed like an eternity for help, before he was pulled aboard the *Lord Collingwood*, where his sodden clothes were removed, he was given a dry blanket and a hot cup of tea. As dawn began to break, the trawler came upon two figures in duffel coats standing on wreckage breaking the surface. It was the captain, Commander Elliott, and the chief boatswain's mate who had climbed to the highest point in the superstructure, the roof of the bridge, as the *King Orry* began to go down. They were picked up by the trawler with not much more than wet feet. Around 2 am the ship rolled onto her side, but as she was resting on a sandbar, tidal action later righted her and a famous photo exists of the *Tynwald* steaming past the funnel and mast of the *King Orry*, protruding from the water.

Not everyone was as fortunate as Hayes and Jones, and among the missing presumed dead was 24-year-old Ward

Attender James Lee of Bootle; he had previously sailed as a fireman with the Merchant Navy, but had joined the Royal Navy upon the outbreak of war. Lee is now buried at Etaples Military Cemetery near Boulogne, some considerable distance from Dunkirk. As casualties were normally interred at the closest available cemetery, one may presume that his body drifted with the current and washed up further down the coast. Another crewman, Stoker Fred Buckingham from east London, dived into the water as she went down – the third ship to have been sunk from under him so far in this war. Of the four Manxmen among her crew – engineers Stanley Cowley, Laurence L. Quine, Griff Hughes and J.R. Scarffe – all escaped with their lives, and Scarffe was able to jump into a boat which came alongside so that he did not even get his clothes wet! One of the other Manx engineer officers, Griff Hughes was not so lucky and was injured. He wrote to his wife from Dover Casualty Hospital:

> As you see I am at Dover – there is no need to worry, as I have only been hit in the left shoulder & will be moved on soon I hope. The ship's been blown to pieces & I don't know anything about the others, as I was picked up off a raft.[37]

So bad did the bombing of ships at Dunkirk become that on 29 May Admiral Ramsay took the decision to withdraw the eight most modern destroyers in the evacuation fleet – it was simply too risky to continue to expose them to danger. Three had already been sunk and six damaged. Never the less the unarmed ships of the Merchant Navy were still expected to enter the inferno of Dunkirk.

The *Lady of Mann* was another modern vessel, constructed for the company in 1930 by Vickers-Armstrongs of Barrow-in-Furness. She was ordered to mark the centenary of the company, and was said to have been 'foreman-built' as at the height of the depression most of the yard hands had been laid off and only the most senior and experienced workmen were retained. This was reflected in the splendour of her internal fixtures and fittings. The largest vessel ever built for the company, she was 3,104 tons in weight, had a length of 360 feet, beam of 50 feet and a speed of 23 knots. She was regarded as the flagship of the fleet, and carried out sterling work in the Dunkirk operations. Bill Cheall of the Green Howards was one of the many thousands of troops evacuated by her. He remembered the vast lines of British soldiers waiting patiently in the dunes for their turn to board one of the rescue ships:

> There was always the hot headed lad who thought he had more right to get away, but the officers only had to draw a revolver and they calmed down and accepted the inevitable. In the prevailing mood of many of the men it was common to see groups of soldiers kneeling down, being led by a Padre, in prayer.
>
> There by the side of the jetty, a ship was waiting to be loaded with human cargo. We walked along the wooden

pier and back came the planes – it seemed never ending – trying to bomb our ship but without success. We walked along for about a half-mile to the ship we would be boarding. Miraculously, the Mole was still intact, but there was a six-foot gap in the planking where a bomb had gone through without exploding and loose planks had been put across. Another thirty yards and we came to our ship. At the top end of a gangway stood an officer, counting soldiers as they went aboard.

The ship was a ferry ship called the *Lady of Mann* (how could I forget that name?). How lucky we considered ourselves to be; out of all those thousands of men, we were being given the opportunity to be evacuated. It was almost impossible for men of the same companies to stay together, but that was no consequence at a time like this.

The ferry was fast becoming packed with grateful lads. The Captain would know how many men the ship could carry, but God alone knows what would have happened had a bomb hit us! I was lucky enough to be on deck to see what was happening and it must have been very claustrophobic down below deck. I kept my eyes on the nearest Carley float in case the worst happened. The fact that we had managed to get on a boat was no guarantee that we would reach England because the Luftwaffe was doing its utmost to prevent us. As the ship was filling up, a Padre came and stood on a ladder, called for silence and prayed for our deliverance to England. At last, packed like sardines, the ship started to tremble and, so very slowly, we pulled away from the Mole - it was 1800 hrs.[38]

One of her crew was Stanley Shimmin, who had been with her since she was launched. As she was loading troops, bombs fell all around her. Shimmin recalled:

One of them fell very close to the '*Lady*'. We had a look over the side but we couldn't see any damage so we went to Folkestone to discharge the troops. As the troops were leaving the ship we wondered why a crowd of people were looking down at the stern, so we leaned over the side and saw that one of the plates was pouring out water like a pepperbox. The bomb blast must have splintered through the plates but it must have been in a water-tight compartment, for it was not until the troops came off at Folkestone and the ship rose higher in the water did we realise we had any damage.[39]

Tynwald and *Lady of Mann* both carried far more troops than their Board of Trade official capacity allowed. Aboard the *Tynwald*, a number of crew members were decorated for making repeated crossings into the war zone. Among these were Alan Watterson the chief officer, who was awarded the Distinguished Service Cross, and one of the sailors,

Tom Gribben who was awarded the Distinguished Service Medal. The Radio Officer C.R. Mason was also awarded the Distinguished Service Cross. The Donkeyman James Allan and the purser aboard the *Tynwald,* William Lister, were both mentioned in dispatches. Lister was a student at a teacher training college in 1939 and had taken the purser's role as a summer job. When the Steam Packet fleet went to war, he went with it. He left a marvellous account of his own experiences in 1940. Just before Dunkirk he and Albert Corkish, who was purser on the *Fenella* were on a week's leave in the Isle of Man. When they got back to Southampton, they found that the ships had left for Dover. Here Corkish found the *Fenella,* but the *Tynwald* had already moved on again to Deal. Lister told him that he was a lucky man to have found his ship, shook hands and set off in search of his own vessel. Two days later Corkish was dead, killed in the bombing of the *Crested Eagle.* Lister reached *Tynwald* and boarded her just as she was about to set off for Dunkirk:

> I was busy paying the crew, I decided to pay out that night, I was that busy with the figures catching up, that I didn't look outside. Eventually I went out on deck, Lord bless my soul, it was like being in Hades, because there were fires everywhere, you could see the troops lining up along the beach, planes overhead, it was seven o clock in the evening and that was my introduction to Dunkirk. Ships were virtually queuing up to go into the harbour: We didn't take them off the beaches, we

had nothing to do with that, that had to be small craft. We went alongside the mole, the old wooden mole and there weren't any bollards, you just had to tie up as best you could. Next morning I went on my second trip. While those poor devils were over there it was our bounden duty to go and get them. By this time though we were really saddened as the *Mona's Queen* had been sunk by a mine. The best thing though was not to think about it...[40]

He was to encounter the sunken *Fenella*, the ill-fated ship of his friend, on one of his own crossings:

We were going into the Mole at Dunkirk and were exactly alongside the wreck, which was half out of the water, when we grounded. An old seaman on board panicked and said, 'They were built together and they will perish together.' However *Tynwald* refloated with the high tide and after Dunkirk went on to take part in evacuations further down the coast.[41]

Also aboard the *Tynwald* as a junior engineer was Harry Crawley, the son of Mr and Mrs J. Crawley of 'Woodside', Four Roads, Port St Mary. He wrote in 2008:

On the approach to Dunkirk we passed destroyers, naval trawlers, cross channel ships, including those of the Southern Railway, Great Western Railway and

LNER, all of which were crowded with troops. Nearing Dunkirk we saw the town afire and the troops crowding the beaches. We berthed at the innermost berth of the jetty with shells bursting just short of us. The tide was low and it was not possible to get the gangways out, but luckily the ship possessed 14lb sledge hammers and we managed to break the concrete railings. We loaded troops and were overloaded according to the rules, but who worried about rules then.

On the next trip to Dunkirk we had to go into the harbour side of the jetty and we passed a trawler slowly sinking. We loaded French soldiers (they were some of the last to leave Dunkirk) and I will never forget Mr Tommy Cain on the jetty waving an iron rod and shouting 'vite, vite'; he was a great brave man, a DSC from World War One. This was my last run from Dunkirk and I was pretty stressed out, like the rest. The Chief Engineer had earlier become so stressed that he was unable to move and had to be led ashore by medics; he was later replaced by Mr Tom Vickers who was 2nd Engineer on the *Viking*.[42]

Crawley remembered that as they passed the *Fenella* he could see straight away that she was sunk at her mooring; the lifeboat davits were out on the port side, but there was no lifeboat there. Also, the sea was up to her shelter deck, and she was 9 or 10 feet lower in the water than she should have been. For him it was the lack of sleep which was the most difficult aspect of the evacuation.

Among the British troops rescued by *Tynwald* was Londoner Wilf Bradley, nominally a Royal Artillery signaller but now part of 'Macforce', a composite unit of stragglers from infantry and anti-tank units. Arriving at Dunkirk their officer marked out squares on the beach and the men excavated a foxhole each using their tin helmets; here they waited for three days without food until the ship arrived alongside the Mole. Then they boarded, under shellfire, and crossed to Dover. He remembered that upon disembarkation the troops received the luxury of an apple and a bar of chocolate each. Another soldier who came back on the *Tynwald* was Sergeant Ted Pierce of the 61st Medium Regiment, Royal Artillery, from Llanrwst, Conwy. Sun-tanned, and showing little sign of the ordeal he had gone through, once home he told a local journalist of his escape from France with his comrades:

> As we neared the coast we were ordered to blow up our guns and barricade the roads and to make as quickly as possible for Dunkirk. After a long walk about we saw Dunkirk burning furiously in the distance and I thought there was very little hope of getting away. But I counted without the Royal Navy and the help from the Merchant Navy and every other type of craft one could think of. In fact, there was a pretty regular service over the Channel.[43]

On 30 May the evacuation was greatly aided by the weather; it was foggy and overcast which restricted enemy air activity, the Luftwaffe being grounded for much of the day. It was no coincidence that the largest single number of troops evacuated were taken out on this date, however on 31 May the weather cleared again, and losses from the Luftwaffe reached a peak on 1 June when thirty-one Allied ships were sunk by air attack. Thomas Cannell was a junior engineer aboard the *Ben-My-Chree*. He remembered:

> Friday 31st May we sailed to Dunkirk. Like so many days of the summer of 1940, it was beautifully sunny and calm. I had been in the dining saloon for dinner, so it was past mid-day when I came on deck, and found that we had already reached Dunkirk. A huge column of smoke was rising from the burning fuel tanks, but everything was so much quieter than I expected – somehow I had thought that there would be the continual sound of battle. We were standing off the harbour entrance – I suppose we were awaiting instructions to go alongside the Mole. A destroyer was standing quite near to us, and a naval rating was amusing himself by whistling in imitation of the sound of a falling bomb. We were to hear the real thing soon enough. We had approached Dunkirk from the west, and were moving very slowly and were close in. There were wrecks of ships all around, but closer inshore a sunken ship was sitting upright with much of her

superstructure above water. We at once recognised her as the *King Orry*...

The *Ben-My Chree* slowly drifted past the harbour entrance, past the East Mole. There at the end berth on the outside of the East Mole lay the *Fenella*. At first glance, there seemed to be nothing wrong with her, except that there was no activity on the ship, and she seemed unusually low in the water. Then we realised she was sunk at her berth, and we wondered what had happened to her crew. Three ships lost out of the small Manx fleet on war service that we knew of – what about the other ships? The morale of the crew was badly shaken.[44]

It seems however that not every member of the crew was as perturbed by the situation. Second Lieutenant Frank Proudfoot of the Royal Artillery was among those who boarded the ship, exhausted and thirsty. He headed for the saloon, where he asked the Manx steward for whisky, perhaps to steady his nerves. The barman's laconic reply has gone down in folklore, and convinced Proudfoot that with this kind of stoicism Britain could not possibly lose the war:

Sir we are not allowed to open the bar whilst the ship is in port.[45]

None the less the two days of intense bombing and air attack in Dunkirk had clearly affected others on the *Ben-My-Chree*.

Today it is well known that every individual has a finite store of courage, and in repeated exposure to danger at some point a person's nerve will break. For some people this point will be reached sooner than for others. Thomas Cannell continued:

> On a ship there is no place where one can take cover from bombing but it seemed to me that by staying on the main deck, with the top deck above me, the risk of being hit by bomb fragments was reduced. Perhaps there was another advantage in this – I couldn't see the bombers coming in to attack, but the explosions of the bombs sounded extremely close. So, during the afternoon the ship was gradually filling up with men. Some soldiers had filled their water bottles with wine ... but there seemed to be no hurry to get the ship away from the Mole and out to sea. In dangerous situations, one tries to rationalise the dangers, but there seemed to me to be an inexorable logic in that if the shop lay alongside the mole and was continually dive bombed, eventually one bomb must score a direct hit. After all, we were a sitting duck, like an aunt sally at a fairground, not even a machine gun with which to fire back ... the ship would be at least three hours taking troops aboard. In the boiler room that night, as the ship lay at Folkestone, I recall thinking to myself 'Surely they can't send us back into that Hell a second time!' But of course they did, and the next day we were crossing the Channel again to Dunkirk.[46]

One of the older hands aboard the *Ben* was John William Hawkins, from Glen Chass, who was 53 years of age at this time. He had started his maritime career in sailing vessels, and had been with the ship since it was launched in 1927. He remembered:

> I was in her all the war, in Dunkirk twice, the last time I went to Dunkirk, we were by ourselves, the destroyers was coming on in, and taking the troops we had, [saying] 'Come on, you'll be in England sooner than on that thing.' And they were taking them off instead of guarding us while we were in, because we had nothing only a little gun on the top, they should have been in guarding us while we were in. And we were left alone in, only ourselves waiting for stragglers coming down off the beach, and there was two boats went out ahead of us, one was a boat called the *Scotia*, used to run from Holyhead to Kingstown, and another little French boat went out ahead of us full up, and we were saying, 'My God, there's them boats gone out, and we're left here alone.' They dropped two bombs on us, but they went each side of the pier, and so we got away, and when we got out these two boats that went out ahead of us was sunk, and the old *Mona's Isle* one of the Isle of Man boats was picking up survivors. And there was shells dropping ahead of us, shells dropping in front of us, but we got away ... I had some narrow shaves.[47]

The 'gun on the top' to which Hawkins makes reference was actually a Holman Projector, a Heath-Robinson device intended for lobbing grenades upwards at attacking aircraft. That on the *Ben* was damaged on its first journey, when vibration from the ship's engines caused its compressed air supply to leak away. So infatuated was the Royal Navy by this device, that they actually cancelled the *Ben*'s first scheduled run to Dunkirk, sending her instead to Portsmouth to have it repaired. The *Scotia* which Hawkins saw go under was a former London Midland Scottish Railway steamer, commandeered as a troop transport. She was sunk on 1 June with the loss of thirty of her crew. It was estimated that some 300 French troops on board also perished in this incident. Seeing companion ships stricken in this way greatly unnerved many of the civilian crews on other vessels involved in the evacuation.

Among the soldiers waiting to embark, the situation was equally stressful. Reg Bazeley of the Royal Engineers had been waiting patiently on the beach, even playing impromptu games of football between the air raids to break the tension, until:

> Then on 31st May we were ordered to join the lines. We were told to destroy anything that would be an encumbrance to us, and to take mainly what we stood in, weight and space being the order of priority. Some of the chaps had smuggled pet dogs along with them but many of these were being thrown back on to the beach or into the sea. Two more boats, one an Isle of

Man packet steamer named '*Tynwald*' and another named '*Ben My Chree*' filled up and pulled away. We waited and went on waiting. Movement was so slow that once again fear of not reaching a boat began to take over. Fear that the boat would fill before we got on to it. Fear of impending air raids.

Another vessel the '*Lady of Mann*' slipped away, and then I was hauled aboard the '*Manxman*'. I have never appreciated anything so much as I did that mug of thick sweet cocoa that was shoved into my hand! This was IT. We were finally aboard. All we had to do now was pray. I remember thinking, 'Please God let the bombers miss us.' It was 31st May, and suddenly I remembered it was my 22nd birthday! Packed like sardines in a can with shouts of 'hang on' we sidled away, skirting the protecting naval ships that were firing ceaselessly. We were on our way to Dover.[48]

Another account comes from Second Lieutenant Humphrey Bredin of the Royal Ulster Rifles. His battalion had seen hard fighting on the retreat to Dunkirk, but arrived at the Mole intact and in good order. Bredin recalled:

When we got down to the Mole at Dunkirk, the Commanding Officer had said I understand there is a boat there which could take most of us if not all of us, and we saw moored alongside the Mole, a ship that was rocking too and fro most of the time, because there were bombs dropping in the harbour, but we started getting on board. There was a dead man lying across the gang plank and we stepped over him fairly gingerly, and I gradually managed to get my company sort of into little corners, sitting down somewhere and got them reasonably comfortable, and then I sat down myself somewhere in a corner; this was an Isle of Man paddle [sic] steamer called the *Ben my Chree*. When I saw it first I thought to myself, 'I don't know how on earth it has got here, and I doubt if it will be able to get back,' it didn't look terribly sort of seaworthy, however it did get back. We got back without remembering much, I think we just slept, I suppose if the boat had been sinking we would have realised and woken up.[49]

Tom Corteen was aboard the *Manxman* (under her Captain P.B. Cowley) and his crew were now as shaken as those on the *Ben*:

In the evacuation of Dunkirk, I was both mate and second mate of the *Manxman* for the whole week. This was because the original mate had a nervous breakdown on the first run over to Dunkirk, so I had everything to see to and organise ... some vessels would be in and out of Dunkirk in two or three hours if the troops were there in great numbers. So it was the actual time spent in the place that mattered, not the number of times in and out. The tension would ease every time one was leaving the place as it was in and around Dunkirk where all the action was taking place.

Another day we were on the point of leaving with a full load of troops after being alongside for about four hours, when some of the crew (who had been standing by to let go) came running to me in a very disturbed state. A destroyer had tied up alongside us and our troops were naturally swarming down on board her. She took nearly all of them, in fact she had to cast off or she would have been overwhelmed.

I told the destroyer commander what I thought about it all, the way he had upset my crew after what they had been through. They were in and out in minutes and we now had to wait alongside for hours again, awaiting troops who had to be rounded up and sent down the mole to us. No troops were left exposed on the mole unless there was a vessel alongside to receive them. This destroyer left us, the only vessel in, nothing even outside the pierheads. We were alone with no protection, not even a pop-gun, not a single tin hat amongst us, in fact, no soldier would even lend me his tin hat. When I had to go forward to pin the bow rudder whilst we were lying alongside, Hugh Crennell, the lamp trimmer (who had been a Lewis gunner in the 1914-18 war) procured a Lewis gun and ammunition from one of the troops. I helped him to set it up, foreside of the bridge deck and also helped to load with practically all tracer bullets. He used that gun a few times before we got away. And he was certainly turning a few Stukas off course, I could see bullets passing right through the Stukas. I did not even realise that they were probably machine gunning us as well. Without that gun, I am sure we would never have got out of Dunkirk, but Lamps had cracked up on the passage [back] and had to be put ashore.

... I had not slept for a week, my nerves were keeping me going.[50]

Corteen was finally taken off the ship and replaced by a regular naval officer the next day, 2 June 1940. At times since then, controversy has resurfaced in connection with the so called 'mutinies' and refusals by crews of some Steam Packet vessels to sail to Dunkirk that day. However, little of what has been written is based on fact. It is necessary to examine the reactions and motives of some of the crews of the *Ben-My-Chree* and *Tynwald* in particular, who have been tarred with this brush of mutiny, and to try to understand them. When requested by the Admiralty to make a third trip to Dunkirk, the master of the *Ben-My-Chree* Captain George Woods wrote back: 'I beg to state that after our experience in Dunkirk yesterday my answer is No.'[51]

In fact, the ship had already been damaged by bombing, and there was every chance she would be hit again if she went back into Dunkirk without air cover. The master of the

Tynwald, Captain Qualtrough, who was 63 years of age, sent back a similar reply, stating:

> Our crews have been continually on their feet all week and especially the deck officers who have had to be on their feet for so long. I myself have had 4 hours sleep for the week and am at present physically unfit for another trip like we have had ... There are two more of the crew going ashore now absolutely nervous wrecks and certified by both the Army and Naval doctor.[52]

Even younger men were not immune to the effects of stress and trauma. One of the greasers aboard the *Tynwald*, 23-year-old James Greggor from Market Street, Peel returned to his sister's home in Fleetwood after the evacuation, suffering from nerves, and was then diagnosed by his own local doctor with shell shock. Greggor had been sunk already in the war, when his trawler was torpedoed. On that occasion he was rescued from the water, also suffering from shock.

There is no doubt that the Steam Packet crews had been extremely shaken, both by their own experiences and by the effect on morale of the loss of the *Mona's Queen*. Although the Royal Navy was still expecting the merchant ships to enter Dunkirk, it now considered the port now too dangerous to risk its own destroyers there! It is also important to bear in mind that the refusals to return to Dunkirk were not confined to the IOMSPCo. The crew of the *Canterbury* were so badly traumatised that the ship could not continue to play a part. The master of the LNER steamer *Malines* considered the risk to his ship so great, and his crew so shaken, that without orders he left Dover and returned to his home port of Southampton. Several south coast lifeboats also refused to return. The master of the Channel Islands ferry *St Helier* made a similar decision. In some sensationalist press articles, the Steam Packet crews have even stated to have been forced back on to their ships at bayonet point! Thomas Cannell remembered the events of 2 June 1940:

> I was more scared during those two days of bombing than I was during all my subsequent years at sea in the following war years. Sometime during the late afternoon, the Chief Engineer T.W. Craine asked me if I were willing to volunteer to stay with the ship on another sailing to Dunkirk. I asked him if he or the Second Engineer George Clague were staying and he said 'No'. At this, I said I wouldn't stay either. I can't recall after this passage of time if the Chief said specifically that Captain George Woods had decided, on the experience of the past two days, that he would not sail, but that seemed to be the general impression. The Chief told me to pack my bags quickly, as the ship was going alongside, and the crew would be leaving. So where was the alleged 'insurrection' or 'mutiny'?
>
> I did indeed pack my two bags quickly – I had to leave some things like books, and a teapot etc behind as there

was no room for them. My room was on the main deck – and on the same side as the gangway, so not much that happened would miss my attention. Yes I saw Naval guards on the quayside, but that seemed normal to me as the withdrawal was a Naval operation. I did not see any bayonets – indeed I would have felt angry to see them as such would be quite unnecessary. One document alleges 'the crew were demonstrating and shouting that they were going to leave the ship.' This is nonsense – the ship specifically came alongside so that any crewmember who had not volunteered to sail again, could disembark, so why would they be demonstrating? My own feeling at the time was that everyone on the quayside was rather quiet – we'd come through two days of hell, and now felt a sense of relief. A murmur did indeed go up when we saw a machine-gun being carried on to the ship – there had been no machine-gun for us.[53]

Lieutenant Commander W.C. Bushell, of HMS *Wivern*, was placed aboard the *Ben-My-Chree* at Folkestone on 2 June and reported:

It was emphasised that I was not to consider myself in command of the ship but to employ all possible means to get her to sail for Dunkirk as a number of the officers and crew were apparently unwilling to do so. Owing to the efforts of the company which owns the ship, and their agent in Folkestone, this presented no difficulty whatsoever ... all men unwilling to sail had been replaced by others not only willing but eager to sail.[54]

Some of these replacement crewmen came from the *Manx Maid*, which had thus far spent a frustrating week riding at anchor with engine problems, but in the view of many, much more should have been done, both by the IOMSPCo and the Admiralty, to provide relief crews so that the same men were not expected to make repeated trips without sleep or rest, though to be fair to the Steam Packet Company, they were short of experienced sailors. The word 'mutiny' is also iniquitous. Steam Packet Company minutes in the wake of Dunkirk make repeated references to 'refusals to volunteer'. This is a contradiction in terms; one can be asked to volunteer, but no blame should attach if one is not able for whatever reason to do so. As one member of the Merchant Navy stated, 'we suffered one of the highest casualty rates of the war, yet we were constantly being told by the authorities that we were civilians!' The word mutiny in the context of what happened at Dunkirk is inappropriate, not to say inaccurate. If experienced Steam Packet captains and crews refused to sail, they would not have done this without good reason. All of the crews had already undertaken at least one trip into Dunkirk and had experienced first-hand being a sitting duck target without any air protection at all. Few born since can have any understanding of what this must have been like, though there is now a better awareness of post traumatic stress. The campaign to pardon those shot for cowardice in the First World War has highlighted the fact that most people have a breaking point, if repeatedly subjected to mortal fear.

In 1940 neither the Admiralty in Dover, nor the directors of the Steam Packet Company who were initially hostile towards the captains who had refused to sail, had any real understanding of what their crews were being asked to do. To some extent the captains were damned if they did, and damned if they didn't, for they were responsible for the safety of the ship which was company property, and it was for them to decide if the risk of damage was too great. Woods was censured by the company for leaving its property in the hands of strangers when the ship was temporarily taken over by the Royal Navy, but one has to ask, what choice did he have? What efforts were made by the company to send a relief crew? Both Woods and Qualtrough were examined by Dr Charles Pantin at the behest of the company, and both were diagnosed as having shell shock, yet the company suspended both of them, along with Cowley of the *Manxman,* immediately after Dunkirk.

Another aspect to bear in mind is that whilst the troops on the beaches were largely in their teens or early twenties, the men on the Steam Packet ships were often much older. The Steam Packet did not introduce a pension scheme until 1938 and it was not uncommon to find men sailing well into their sixties. Time and again when looking at crew members we find them in their fifties at Dunkirk. This is a significant factor – these were married men with families, and many of them had already been through the First World War. The naval officer who was placed aboard *Tynwald*, summed up the situation in his report with the words:

> I feel it right to remark that most of the officers and ratings of *Tynwald* who declined to sail for Dunkirk were elderly men who had already been there and were possibly shaken by the sight of their sister ship *Fenella*, sunk at the end of the east pier.[55]

It has also been suggested in some quarters that those who did not wish to return to Dunkirk had political motives or were defeatist. This is unlikely, and the simplest answer is probably true, that all of these men had been through an experience scarcely imaginable – some of them more than once, and they had simply had enough. Many had reached a point of physical and nervous exhaustion.

Part of the problem lay in the very differing traditions and approaches of the Royal and Merchant navies. Admiral Ramsay was frequently frustrated by the actions of the merchant crews and in his Dispatch reported that as of 1 June he had placed ratings and a naval officer aboard all of the personnel ships at Dunkirk. There was a culture clash between the impersonal, rules based disciplinary structure of the Royal Navy and the much more personal and reciprocal approach within the merchant fleet. They ran by virtue of consent, and the authority of a master did not extend beyond the conclusion of any particular voyage.

Recently, however, the research of Manx historian David Kneale has revealed a stunning new twist in this saga. Information contained within a previously closed file at the Isle of Man Public Record Office shows that the Island's lieutenant governor in 1940, Vice-Admiral Lord Granville, an ex-Royal Navy officer, had taken a keen interest in the events at Dunkirk. Letters reveal that he was in direct personal contact with Admiral Ramsay and others shortly after the events. Lest it be in any doubt how much sway Granville still held in the Royal Navy, it should be remembered that, in addition to having been an equerry to the late King George V, his wife was the sister of the former Elizabeth Bowes-Lyon; as the brother-in-law of the Queen of the United Kingdom, his influence went right to the very top of the establishment. The scramble to apportion blame for what had happened in France in 1940, and to appear on the right side of history was already beginning. If disgruntled Merchant Navy crews, as was already beginning to happen, returned to the Isle of Man and began to reveal how poorly the navy had acquitted itself in protecting its mercantile brethren, then a serious scandal might well emerge, and Granville would undoubtedly learn of it. There were those in the navy with reputations to protect, and it seems that the best way to do this was to discredit and smear the Manx boats at Dunkirk with accusations of cowardice or treacherous behaviour. Accordingly, it appears that a document was prepared specifically for Lord Granville which, disguised as a report into the performance of personnel ships across the board, deliberately and maliciously distorted the facts in relation to the vessels from the Isle of

Man Steam Packet Company. A different set of standards was applied to those masters and crews of ships from other companies, not to mention crews of the Royal Navy's own ships, which it was reluctant to admit had also suffered cases of nervous exhaustion.

Granville continued for some months to interfere, pressing for the names of those who had not gone back to Dunkirk and seeking to remove their pension rights. The most appalling illustration of his callous attitude is to be found in a letter of 16 September 1940 where he states:

> If one of the mutinous masters had been shot at Dover and another at Folkestone there would have been no further trouble.[56]

By now, however a fuller picture of what had actually happened was beginning to emerge. On 3 October the Steam Packet board of directors allowed the masters of *Ben-My-Chree*, *Tynwald* and *Manxman* to state their cases in person. For the first time they heard credible first-hand accounts of what had actually happened at Dunkirk. All three masters were promptly re-instated. The company began to resist Granville's further attempts to interfere, and challenged Admiral Ramsay's report. Ramsay was by now back tracking, his letter to the directors being recorded in their minutes:

> Regarding the conduct of Captain Cowley, of the '*Manxman*.' Admiral Ramsay states that in his previous

report he did not intend to convey an impression that the Master had failed personally, his attitude was correct and the difficulties he had to contend with in respect of some of his Engineers and other members of his crew were considerable and may have been outside his control.[57]

Dunkirk however was not the only evacuation from the harbours of northern France. It is a little known fact that troops continued to be evacuated from other ports, notably Le Havre and Brest, for some weeks after Dunkirk, in what were referred to as Operation Aerial and Operation Cycle. Harry Kinley, who had narrowly missed being posted to the ill-fated *Fenella*, remembered participating in these efforts aboard the *Viking*. She was one of the company's oldest ships, completed in 1905 by Armstrong Whitworth and company of Newcastle upon Tyne, the first turbine steamer in the company's fleet. She had been fast in her day and her top speed of 24 knots meant that only the ocean-going Cunard liners *Lusitania* and *Mauretania* were faster, and for many years she held the record for the fastest run from Fleetwood to Douglas, set in 1907. A quirk of her layout meant that this 1,957 ton ship was the only vessel in the Steam Packet fleet to have her first class accommodation aft and her steerage section forward. She had actually seen Royal Navy service in the First World War as a seaplane carrier, but now she was ageing and somewhat obsolete. As a coal burner, with funnels glowing with flame, she was hardly inconspicuous. One of her Royal Navy escorts signalled to her:

> You are a column of smoke by day and a ball of fire by night. You are visible for miles.

Laconically, her crew signalled back:

> We know![58]

Kinley takes up the story once more, with a description of events on 10 June:

> I joined the *Viking* in the dry dock she was in, she'd been in collision with a small Norwegian ship, and we went out but by the time we were ready to take passengers, Dunkirk had finished, there was no one there but we were sent there to the vicinity of Dunkirk, no one knows why because we were a coal burner, about four double ended boilers and you can imagine at night time filling these with coals the flames coming out of the funnels and the smoke. They couldn't have sent a worse ship there, there was nobody in Dunkirk, they had all gone. It was the night Italy had declared war on us and anyhow we got into the harbour area when we got word to go to St Valéry ... Then we got word to proceed immediately to Le Havre. We got into Le Havre and there was hell let loose there and we anchored it a bit

too close to a French man of war battleship, we found that out because Jerry came over and started pelting us from the air, and I could see one plane coming over us and he put a bomb each side of us (straddled us) and then he hit the man of war, and at the stern of us there was a Polish ship...she was converted into a hospital ship and she capsized right over.

We were ordered then into Le Havre to get troops on board immediately and they were all Scottish, and those men had been chased from Dunkirk mind you and we got them on board, and we got the Vice Consul from Dieppe on board too. German planes were going over, and when one went over an officer blew a whistle, and the troops all dropped flat, but we were still all looking around to see what was going on! It was too late we had to get them on board and get out, there was a tug boat towing us off and he was shouting 'Vamoosh vamoosh' because he wanted to get off, he'd got the wind up, because the planes were coming over good and proper, and he went ahead of his ropes and broke the rope, and it got stuck in his propeller.

That morning going up into Southampton water going in through the boom defence – it was a lovely summer morning – and we went in slow and we had to stop for an examination steamer, God knows what for. The Scotsmen were all there, she had a long fo'csle head on her, and there must have been 500 men on that fo'csle head, with all their kits, rifles, gas masks and all that type of thing. The bell went, behind the after funnel (she had two funnels) for breakfast, so they went to get their bully beef. They were wonderful chaps.

The examination boat asked, 'where are you from?' and I said Le Havre, but you were not supposed to name the place, they were from the Navy so I had to say Port 23 or 24 whatever it was. He said, 'Who have you got on board?' I said, 'can't you damn well see who we've got, we've got 3000 troops on board', nearly 4000 actually with all their kit, he said 'have you got any evacuees on board', I said 'aren't we all evacuees?!'[59]

As well as her cargo of soldiers, the master of the *Viking*, Captain Philip 'Ginger' Bridson had brought another souvenir of their Le Havre evacuation back with him. A French soldier who had come on board had given him his bugle. He told Bridson that he had last used it to sound the retreat, and now he was too ashamed of it to continue carrying it. It was to remain a treasured possession for the rest of his life, and is now on display in the Isle of Man Steam Packet gallery at the House of Manannan, Peel. Will Lister was also involved in this operation, with the *Tynwald*. He remembered:

The worst time I ever remember was a whole day's dive-bombing at Le Havre. We were the last troopship out of Le Havre. The *Lady* was with us and the *Viking*. We were mighty tired men I can tell you.⁶⁰

The *Tynwald* carried about 500 men on that last trip from Le Havre, as well as valuable equipment. There were no pilots to guide the ship out through the minefields, so the crew had no choice but to pick their way through as best they could. Lister continues:

> Those poor troops thought they were bound for Blighty but when we were underway we were radioed to take them into Cherbourg to fight again.⁶¹

The *Viking*'s next mission was to St Peter Port, the capital of Guernsey. With the fall of France, the British Channel Islands which were only a few miles off the German-held coast, became indefensible. Churchill conceded that they would have to be abandoned to the enemy, and they became the only British territory to be occupied by the Nazis during the Second World War. Before that happened however, an extraordinary evacuation took place. The people of Guernsey were offered the opportunity of escape for their children. Many reluctantly accepted it, and there were many tearful scenes as the Isle of Man Steam Packet vessel *Viking*, still under her master 'Ginger' Bridson, arrived to collect them. Bridson, from Castletown, was a veteran of the First World War and had worked his way up to the position of master after joining the company as a deck hand. He recalled that taking the children from their families was one of his hardest tasks. For Harry Kinley as well, the unusual mission made a lasting impression upon him:

> We eventually got to St Peter's Port, it was a lovely summer morning, I had been up on the bridge all night, because I was the navigating officer, but we were all dead beat, we had been on our feet for days and we anchored in the North Bay, and the pilot came out, a lobster fisherman, and we were talking to him, I said isn't there a channel that goes out to the north of the island, because we were routed away to the west of the island about twenty miles further than we should have been, aye that's right he said, and he told me. I had this booklet, 'Notice to Mariners' it was issued about twice a week with all the things that had happened in the charts you were sailing in, like buoys being changed and mines being laid, and you had to correct your charts, to know about the waters you were in and I had one of these on the bridge; and I drew this sketch of the route we should take to get round the north side, in pencil on the back of this.
>
> We got into St Peter's Port, alongside the jetty, and it was a beautiful place, here was a sight you would never forget. There were about 1800 children, some of them thought it was wonderful to have a gas mask in a little cardboard box and some sandwiches, half of them had

eaten them by then, about fifty yards beyond them was some barbed wire, and beyond that were the parents. Some of the kids were crying their eyes out, and others thought they were having a wonderful time, running around. There were about 1800 children and the odd nun. Whilst we were loading these children, a woman came staggering aboard. She said, 'Do you want the key to my pub?' She was a Mrs Savage, and it was called the Bull's Head or something. 'You can have it, I'm not going to give it to that bloody Hitler.' I said to Captain Bridson, 'there's a woman here who wants to give you a pub.' 'Don't be so damn silly,' he said. 'I'm Mrs Savage and I own the bloody pub and you can have the bloody thing.' He couldn't of course!

I went down this North Channel that the pilot had showed me, and we saved about an hour's sailing. And off we went to Weymouth, we got there about 1 o'clock in the morning.[62]

Shortly after this, with the loss of its normal summer season traffic, the Steam Packet Company felt that it had no choice but to lay off most of its second mates, Harry Kinley included. He was fortunate however in that he held a Liverpool Pilotage Licence, so was able to obtain a position with the Liverpool Pilotage Service where he remained for the rest of the war, before returning to the company after the close of hostilities.

From 16 June 1940, the British and French began evacuating troops and supplies from Brest, Nantes and St Nazaire. One of the ships involved was the *Manxman*, which after Dunkirk had been ordered to Dartmouth, where she had suffered the indignity of being fired upon by a British guard boat, which had not been informed of her imminent arrival. Now back on war duty, the *Manxman* was also the last British vessel to leave St Malo during the evacuation of that port, and her escape from Cherbourg was one of the most daring recorded during this period, indeed she got away only through the assistance of her accompanying destroyer L11, which fired on a column of Panzer tanks approaching the harbour. Chief Officer Lyndhurst Callow remembered:

> The large cranes along the dockside had been blasted and broken, and were one of the many hazards to shipping. Tanks were approaching the harbour area; the remnants of the Allied armies were fighting them off as best they could. The *Manxman* herself was laden with troops and with stacked ammunition, small arms and even field weapons saved from the catastrophe – one hit from an enemy aircraft could have blown up the entire ship.[63]

There is a long held belief in Steam Packet lore that the German commander Erwin Rommel wrote of a 'cheeky two-funnel steamer'[64] escaping the harbour in a fashion reminiscent of a cork leaving a bottle, a reference to the *Manxman* in the above incident, though it must be stated that the present writer has been unable to substantiate this up to this time, through reference to Rommel's known published works. The *Tynwald* likewise participated in the evacuation of the western French ports after Dunkirk, following which the ship was used to transport German prisoners of war from Liverpool to the 'Tail of the Bank' on the Clyde, where they were transferred to troopships bound for Canada. Her master at this time was Captain Oscar Taylor. Born in 1892, he joined the Isle of Man Steam Packet Company in 1912. He was also in command of the *Manxman* during her time in the Calais evacuation. Harry Crawley remembered that when the prisoners came on board the *Tynwald*, they were not particularly heavily guarded, as once at sea they would have little chance of escape.

The *Manx Maid* had not taken any part in the Dunkirk evacuation, due to engine problems. Becalmed at Dover, her crew had spent an uncomfortable week lying at anchor. Her stores had run out, and the men had spent three days living on arrow root biscuits and ginger snaps. Her fresh water also ran low and the crew had none available for washing. With the engines stopped, there was also no light available in the lower decks. Once back in service she was despatched to Southampton, and crossed to St Malo. However, the port was already under enemy occupation by the time she arrived, and unable to go into the harbour, she returned to England. Her second trip was to Brest, and she picked up nearly 3,000 troops (almost twice her peace-time capacity), waiting by the pier all day. Because she was so low in the water, she developed condenser trouble and had to wait off shore for three hours for calmer weather, before she eventually reached the safety of Plymouth harbour.

After this, she moved to Milford Haven, in company with some of her sister ships from the Steam Packet fleet. We catch a glimpse of one of the Manx ships at Pembroke Dock, during the days following the Channel coast evacuations, in the *Diaries of Evelyn Waugh*. Waugh of course was a prolific writer, best known for the novel *Brideshead Revisited*. He was at this time serving as a captain in the Royal Marines, and although the unit had not served in France it was held in readiness for other operations. He wrote a description of the ship, in his usual caustic and haughty style, under the date 4 July 1940:

> At the end of the week we got orders to move again, marched to Neyland Ferry on Sunday morning and embarked in a small, dirty ship the *Lady of Mann*, where we lived in gross squalor at six hours' notice to sail. Another ship, *St Briac*, has been moved alongside us and has relieved the crowding slightly ... We had a night ashore, greatly incommoded in all arrangements by the Flemish drifters which are our only connection with the shore, but a fairly good time was had by all.[65]

Later Waugh's battalion was disembarked, and continued its training in Cornwall. It was most likely required for home defence, because as August 1940 drew on the people of

Britain prepared for what seemed like an inevitable German invasion. For now at least, the conflict would shift into the skies as the RAF and Luftwaffe fought the Battle of Britain, a struggle for dominance of the airspace over the English Channel. Without this measure of control, the Germans were not foolhardy enough to commence an amphibious assault, even if they had already started assembling barges for their invasion, code named Operation Sealion. As the Royal Navy expanded its operations, new roles would be found for the chartered Steam Packet ships, and indeed additional auxiliary naval vessels would need to be found from within their ranks, to supplement the fleet. This was particularly true in home waters, with the navy's newest and best assets soon to be deployed to the Pacific in increasing numbers.

Chapter Three

Royal Navy Service

In a time of national emergency, converting Merchant Navy vessels into warships was sometimes a quicker way of supplementing the Royal Navy's assets than commissioning new builds. With shipyards working at full capacity in any case, this was an easier way to procure vessels for what might be termed 'second line' or supplementary naval duties. Although they were not heavily armoured or well defended, converted passenger ships often had an impressive turn of speed, and there was a long tradition in the Royal Navy of utilising them as auxiliary cruisers in time of war.

In 1941 the *Viking*, whilst not actually commissioned in the Royal Navy, was taken over by the Admiralty and fitted out for the ill-starred raid on Dieppe in 1942. Captain Jack Holkham was in charge of the ship at this time, with his Chief Officer Lyndhurst Callow. In the event the *Viking* was not actually employed at Dieppe, and was sent instead to Crail on the east coast of Scotland for work with the Fleet Air Arm, in the training of air crews. On different occasions she rescued six airmen whose craft had crashed into the sea. During this time, there was the inevitable confusion with mail, as the ship was sometimes referred to erroneously as HMS *Viking*. There was already a ship of this name in the

Royal Navy, and all personnel accommodated on the Steam Packet vessel (civilian and naval) were instructed to inform relatives that mail should be clearly addressed to SS *Viking*. After seven months, when this job was completed, Holkham received the thanks of the air commander-in-chief for his efficient co-operation.

HMS *Mona's Isle* had been on Royal Navy work since the outbreak of war. Severely damaged at Dunkirk, she was afterwards repaired and then went on to serve as an anti-aircraft protection ship in the region between the rivers Tyne and Forth. We catch a glimpse of her in December 1941 in a letter from Robert 'Battling' Holmes, who had survived the sinking of the *Fenella* and *Crested Eagle*, and was now serving aboard this vessel. He had written to the Manx newspapers asking for readers to send gramophone records; apparently the ship already had a gramophone, but many of its records had been broken in recent rough weather. Holmes also mentioned that entertainment was limited on board and also asked for a dartboard. In a later letter he acknowledged receipt of the dartboard, and added that he had kept his pugilistic skills sharp by entering an inter-service boxing competition, and had knocked out an army opponent in the first round. Apparently there were thirty-nine Manxmen on board; Holmes by this point must have joined the Royal Navy, because in the letter he is referred to as 'stoker', the Royal Navy equivalent of the Merchant Navy's 'fireman.'

The *Mona's Isle* was mainly involved in North Sea convoy escort duties, acting as 'leader', until in 1943 she sustained serious damage and nearly sank, after being rammed in thick fog. The resultant hole in the starboard side near the bow was enormous, and the best part of the ship was submerged as a result of this accident. This Royal Navy auxiliary ship was only able to reach the Tyne after emergency repairs, and even then, she had to reverse into the river to minimise the water pressure against the damaged area. Later in the war she became an accommodation ship for naval ratings, and up until this time her captain was Commander John Hamilton Blair RNR who was an ex-submariner and well known Antarctic explorer (there are two mountains near the South Pole named after him, Mount Hamilton and Mount Blair). In 1942, a journalist in Newcastle upon Tyne reported:

> Strolling along the quayside of a North-East port I meet an old acquaintance! I step back to admire her but she does not recognise me as I touch the brim of my hat – once she sported fun and games. Her decks were filled with laughing carefree holiday-makers, girls in tantalising seaside rigouts and youths clad in spotless flannels. Those days are gone. She is altered this little grey lady the Admiralty has dressed in a quiet uniform. In days of peace the SS *Mona's Isle* was a frivolous little thing in a white and black gown – with two bright red funnels with bracelets of black. She used to carry lads and lasses from across the Irish Sea to the holiday Isle of Man. Maybe you have made her acquaintance. See her to-day. She proudly flies the White Ensign as RN

Auxiliary Cruiser *Mona's Isle*, flak ship on escort duty and patrol. She's carrying guns instead of girls, fully armed against the enemy that strikes from above, upon and beneath the waves. Watchful, day in night out, a ceaseless vigil in storm and tempest, through fog and mist, and the blackness of night, ever prepared for instant action, taking risks hourly to watch and ward the merchant ships sailing in convoy, she cuts through the North Sea, shepherding her flock. Come with me aboard again. Meet the man in charge. Short alert and of quiet voice is Commander John Hamilton Blair DSC RD RNR, from north of the Tweed. He's 45, served in the Antarctic under Sir Douglas Mawson; served five years in submarines in the World War, one with Sir Max Horton 'ace' submarine officer, back to serve in the North Atlantic to capture enemy ships, to sink U-boats, one after a two hour fight, to bring home to port a ship carrying valuable cargo which had lost her rudder, to take command of the good old *Mona's Isle*. Privileged with the run of the ship I meet the Chief Engineer Kelly from the Isle of Man, christened Henry and nicknamed Uncle Harry which rather hits him off.

The funnels are covered in patches, 'like couple pepper pots' says Uncle Harry. Water tanks have been holed by shells and she bears scars of many an action. Twice *Mona's Isle* went to the beaches of Dunkirk and brought back 1600 gallant lads to safety. Many a near miss has shaken this Queen of the sea – she's been badly holed. Nazi planes have swooped down to machine gun her deck, as she has stood by during attacks on her charges with her guns pelting away. In the mess hangs a relic, the ship's megaphone holed like a colander. She boasts a grand crew of officers and men, and she's still a 'happy' ship. And she's 37 years old now this pleasure steamer, turned man o'war ... troopship in the last war ... sunk at Folkestone and righted again to sail once more to the Isle of Man. Night after night through all the tempers of the weather the *Mona's Isle* is at action stations. 'On Victory day' says 'Uncle Harry,' 'we're going to sail up the Mersey again and away with lights aglow to the Isle of Man.' May I be with them ... and until then, salute to brave men and a gallant ship, RN Auxiliary Cruiser *Mona's Isle*.[1]

She was returned to the Isle of Man Steam Packet Company in 1945, lacking her mainmast. The *Manxman* meanwhile was commissioned as HMS *Caduceus* in October 1941, and in this guise she was to serve as a radio detection finding ship. The vessel had been purchased by the Steam Packet Company in 1920 to replace losses in the First World War. Ironically she was acquired from the Admiralty, who in turn had requisitioned her from the Midland Railway Company, which had operated her on the Heysham-Douglas route. She was built by Vickers at Barrow-in-Furness and completed in 1904, and in 1921 she was converted by the Steam Packet

Company to burn oil rather than coal (thus making her the first ship in the company's history to use this fuel). This would undoubtedly have improved her speed, which had been noted by the Royal Navy during her period of First World War service as too slow.

Ordered to her home port of Douglas, she linked up with one of the early radar training stations – HMS *Valkyrie* which was installed on Douglas Head, and patrolled the Irish Sea while naval personnel were trained in radio direction finding. She twice collided with the Victoria Pier, which moved the Admiralty to declare that Douglas Harbour was unsuitable for a vessel of her size, a bizarre decision given that it was her home port. There is an oblique reference to one of these incidents in *Moon Boots and Dinner Suits*, the memoirs of *Dr Who* actor Jon Pertwee. During the war, Pertwee was posted as a Royal Naval Reserve sub-lieutenant to HMS *Valkyrie*. In the book he makes reference to the fact that on one occasion he was responsible for ramming a Steam Packet vessel into the pier at Douglas. As there would be no reason for a Royal Naval officer to be on the bridge of either the *Rushen Castle* or *Snaefell* at this time, one has to draw the conclusion that the vessel in question was *Caduceus*, though Pertwee draws a discrete veil over the matter and at the time of writing, no further details are available. Whatever the truth, after the second incident she was dispatched to work on her radar training duties out of the Clyde, although this posting was also not to be trouble-free; in February 1943, she was driven ashore near Greenock, in a fierce gale. She was subsequently refurbished, and the name *Manxman* was restored to her.

John William Hawkins of Glen Chass had been aboard the *Ben-My-Chree* taking part in the Normandy landings, until the news of the sudden death of his wife at home reached him, in September 1944. She was only 56, and it seems that this news, combined with the stress that he had been under at Dunkirk and afterwards caused some sort of mental or emotional breakdown. He left the ship after this experience, and remembered in 1971:

> My nerves all went and I had to get out of it. So I came home and I had only been home a few days, when the Second Mate that was in the *Ben*, he was home on leave. He was living in Port St Mary, Cubbon his name was, and I was sitting in the house, him and his wife came in. He said, 'Are you comfortable?' I said 'yes, and I'm going to be comfortable too.' He says, 'You're coming to Belfast with me.' I said 'I am not.' He says 'You are, I've told the Super that you're coming with me.' So I said, 'Well you shouldn't have told him, I'm finished.' He said, 'Well I only want two of you for watchmen.' It was the old *Manxman*, and the Navy had her in the wartime, and she was getting ready to go down south again, they were getting her done up to go down. He said, 'I want two of you for watchmen, and you can please yourself when she's ready whether you go in her or not.' Off I goes ... Well I was six, seven months there. I had

nothing to do, we had a Steward waiting on us, and £6 19s a week and [all] found, only at night time one of us would stop aboard and have a look around after the workmen had gone ashore, see if there was any fire or anything, then turn in.

The Mate that was in her then had to go back to the *Ben*, and then there was another fellow came. She was ready then, and he was going to send for his crew. He said to me, 'Are you coming with us?' I said, 'no', he said 'I was going to make you Bosun if you would come with me?' I said 'No I'm not coming.' So he sent for another chap, a fellow by the name of Louis Merryfield of Port Erin, so he came out. So when he was going to send for the rest of the crowd, I thought to myself, there's nothing at home for me, and I was getting alright again, my nerves was clear, so I went to him, 'Have you got all your crew?' He said 'no, why?' I said, 'I think I'll come with you if you'll have me.' Well, he says, 'You're a blooming fool. I was going to make you Bosun, but I can't now because I've sent for him.' I said, 'I wouldn't have a Bosun's job.' He said why, I said 'I'd be only a hand rag for you and a hand rag for the crowd', because I'd have to take all orders from him, and if the crew didn't like it you knew it was me who was going to get the blame, so I said 'no, not me!' So he says, 'Will you take the Lamp Trimmer's job?', you see the Lamp Trimmer had to look after all the deck stores and all.

So I said, 'On one condition on that.' He said 'What's that?' Well I says, 'I was Lamp Trimmer on the *Ben My Chree*, and I had to keep a look out on the Bridge, and my Watch on deck the same as the rest, and I'd turn in after my Watch below and I'd get a knock on my door, somebody wanted something and I'd have to get out and give it to them.' 'Nothing like that here,' he said, 'You're a Dayman. The only time I want you out at night is if we are coming to anchor, I want either you or the Bosun, whoever's Watch it is, I want one of you with me.' 'Right', I said, 'I'll go'. So I went down there, and we were running Calais to Dover.[2]

Having reverted to her old name, *Manxman* then returned to her previous duties as a troopship. Post war she was transferred to the Ministry of War Transport and operated by that body as a troop carrier in the English Channel, then to the British Army of the Rhine, still carrying troops between Harwich and the Hook of Holland. We catch a glimpse of her in a report of a court case from November 1946 when she was operating on trooping duties from Dover:

> Another case of attempting to smuggle cocoa across to the French black market was heard by Dover Magistrates on Friday, when Albert Henry Hartle, of West Bromwich and Frank Thomas Cottage, of Dagenham, both members of the crew of the SS '*Manxman*,' pleaded not guilty to possessing 48 lbs. of cocoa for the purpose of

SS *Mona's Isle* at sea, before the war. Requisitioned into the Royal Navy in 1939 as HMS *Mona's Isle*, she was badly damaged at Dunkirk, but later served as an anti-aircraft ship in the North Sea. (Author's Collection)

SS *Viking* at sea, prior to the war. She took part in the Channel port evacuations of 1940, and also evacuated the children of Guernsey. She was 'a ball of fire by night, and a column of smoke by day.' (Author's Collection)

Above: HMS *King Orry* off Ramsgate, 27 February 1940. This is the only known photo of the ship showing Second World War modifications. (Courtesy of Dave Handscombe)

Below left: A close-up showing gun drill on the aft 12 pounder, HMS *King Orry*. (Courtesy of Dave Handscombe)

Below right: Gun drill on the aft 12 pounder, with 4 inch gun visible at the stern, HMS *King Orry,* April 1940. (Courtesy of Dave Handscombe)

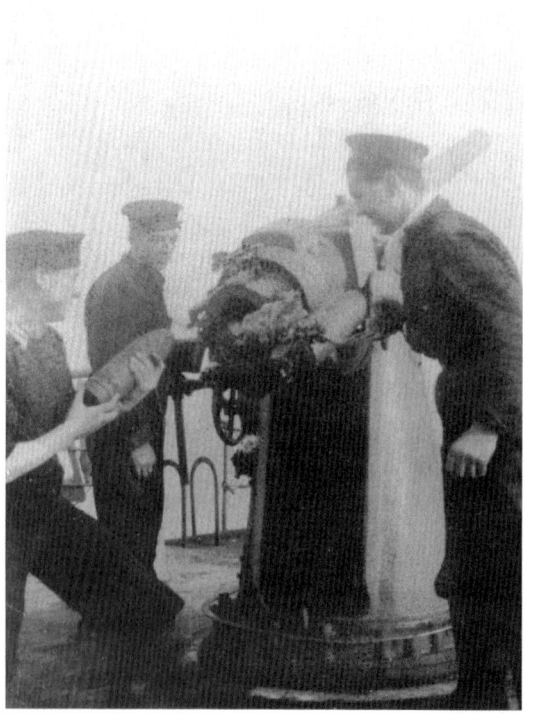

The forward 4 inch gun, mounted on the 'bandstand', HMS *King Orry*. (Courtesy of Dave Handscombe)

Deck-mounted anti-aircraft armament fitted to the *King Orry* when she entered Royal Navy service, a Lewis gun operated by Able Seaman Ray Hughes. (Courtesy of Dave Handscombe)

Above left: Harry Kinley, second officer aboard the *Viking* in 1940. (Author's Collection)

Above right: The Distinguished Service Medal awarded to Bosun Edgerton Watterson, of the transport *Mona's Queen*, for bravery on her second trip to Dunkirk. (Author's Collection)

Mona's Queen sinking after encountering a magnetic mine, 29 May 1940. Dark smoke from the exploding mine can be seen mixing with the lighter coloured steam escaping from her boilers. (Imperial War Museum)

Above: Survivors of the *Mona's Queen* in a lifeboat, shortly after the sinking. (Imperial War Museum)

Right: Chief Officer Bob Clucas of the *Mona's Queen*, who survived the sinking. (Private Collection)

The only survivor of the *Mona's Queen* engine room staff, Lacey Knowles (left) in conversation with the father of one of the junior engineers, who was lost. (Author's Collection)

A TRAGIC STORY.—Fourth engineer L. Knowles, sole survivor of the Mona's Queen's engineers (left) in conversation with Mr. W. Callister, the Steam Packet Co.'s former engineering foreman and father of Assistant Engineer R. C. Callister, who was lost.

NARRATIVE OF S.S. "MANXMAN" 26th May to 4th June 1940.

EVACUATION OF TROOPS AT DUNKIRK.

Monday 27th. Received orders at Southampton to proceed to Dover for orders. 2.15 a.m. arrived off Dover ordered to anchor in Downs. 03.00. anchored in Downs. (28th May).

Tuesday 28th:- Received orders proceed to Dunkirk Weighed anchor 17.55 and proceeded. Grounded 22.50 p.m. on Small sandbank in company with three other boats, precarious position in view of the early rising moon and the possibility of enemy bombing planes. The cause of grounding two buoys marked "lighted" on charts, actually extinguished (cause unknown). 02.30 a.m. 29th refloated- no apparent damage and proceeded to Dunkirk.

06.00. arrived off Dunkirk awaiting berth. Whilst there the "Mona's Queen" Same Co's vessel was blown up by magnetic mine approximately 1000 feet astern of us and sank in four minutes. Two destroyers anchored close by sent two boats off very quickly to the rescue. We had previously passed over the same spot. 8.40 a.m. berthed at Dunkirk. 10.30 a.m. let go. proceeded to Dover for orders. Gunfire and bombing by enemy whilst at the pier, which was replied to by our destroyers and A.A. fire. We had approximate over 2,000 troops on board as we had given all our lifebelts out which number over 2,000. Nothing to report on the passage. Arrived at Dover 16.15 p.m. Received orders proceed to Folkestone. arrived Folkestone 17.35 p.m. disembarked troops.

30th. Took our departure 20.42 p.m. sailed for Dunkirk. Nothing to report during the passage. Arrived off Dunkirk awaiting dawn, and berthed Dunkirk 05.14 a.m. on the 31st. Embarked app. 1700 troops of which 100 were stretcher cases. We were three hours at the pier. Whilst there heavy bombing and shelling by enemy, but our ship escaped damage, our Naval vessels having replied vigorously and drove off the aircraft. 08.15 a.m. sailed from D. voyage without incident- arrived at Folkestone 13.20 p.m. and disembarked the troops.

June 1st. Backed out from Folkestone pier to anchor awaiting orders. Shortly after backing out, a sweeper exploded a magnetic mine not far from Folkestone Pier and in the track which we had previously crossed. This and the "Mona's Queen" incident evidently proved that our "wiping" by the French method at Cherbourg was effective. 19.05 p.m.

A narrative of SS *Manxman* at Dunkirk, prepared by Second Officer Robert Addie, records the loss of *Mona's Queen*. (Courtesy of Robert Addie)

SURVIVORS

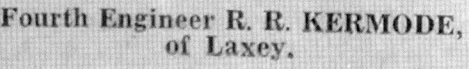

Fourth Engineer R. R. KERMODE, of Laxey.

Fourth Engineer R.R. Kermode of Laxey, who was sunk first at Dunkirk aboard the *Fenella*, and then again aboard the *Crested Eagle*. For the rest of his life he refused to give money to the Red Cross, because at Dover they would only help soldiers and not sunken Merchant Navy men.

Engineer J.E. Corlett who was sunk twice in the same day, firstly aboard the *Fenella* and then aboard the *Crested Eagle*. (Courtesy of the Corlett family)

ENGINEERS MOTION AND JONES, of the Fenella, who were wounded at Dunkirk, the former when the Fenella was hit and the latter when the Crested Eagle, to which he had transferred on the destruction of the Manx boat, was bombed and set on fire.

Engineers Roy Motion and R.W.R. Jones of the *Fenella*. (Author's Collection)

"JOURNEY'S END."—The Fenella lying alongside the east pier at Dunkirk after she had been struck by the bomb which stove in her starboard side. This picture was taken by one of the crew of another Manx vessel which was leaving the port with about 3,000 troops on board.

The stern of the *Fenella* sunk at her berth, alongside the Mole, as viewed by another Steam Packet ship. On the left, lifeboat davits can be seen swung out, and the boat is gone. (Author's Collection)

Engineer Sub-Lieutenant Reg Scarffe, in 1940. He remained aboard the *King Orry* when she became a Royal Navy armed boarding vessel in 1939, and survived the sinking at Dunkirk. (Courtesy of Bernard Scarffe)

Above left: Sub-Lieutenant Godfrey 'Skinny' Hayes (back left, wearing cap) shortly after the sinking of HMS *King Orry* at Dunkirk. (*Starshell* journal of the Royal Canadian Navy)

Above right: Telegraphist E.E. Lane who survived the sinking of *King Orry*. (Author's Collection)

Crew of the yacht *Bystander*, with rescued survivors of HMS *King Orry*.

Lewis gunners aboard *Lady of Mann*, Allan Holding (right) of Wigan, and William Paterson, of Glasgow. Seaman Paterson earned the DSM for bravery at Dunkirk. (Author's Collection)

As the news began to break at home. *Isle of Man Examiner* of 7 June 1940. (Author's Collection)

Right: Major Evelyn Waugh, Royal Marines, who embarked on *Lady of Mann* after Dunkirk.

Below: Manx sailors of Blue Watch, HMS *Mona's Isle*, in 1941. On the extreme left is Stoker Robert 'Battling' Holmes. (Author's Collection)

BLUE WATCH: Back row (left to right)—Leading Stoker G. Cowley (Laxey), Leading Stoker A. McMeiken (Peel), Stoker W. Cannell (Ballasalla), Stoker J. H. Skinner (Ramsey). Middle row (left to right)—Stokers R. Holmes (Douglas), H. Daugherty (Douglas), and J. Joughin (Douglas), Chief Petty Officer J. H. Crennell (Douglas), Stoker E. Gale (Laxey), Front row (left to right)—Stokers M. Murphey (Pulrose Park) and W. J. Cashen (Douglas).

Above left: Able Seaman Ron Hassall, who survived the sinking of HMS *Tynwald*. (Author's Collection)

Above right: Purser Bill Lister who was aboard SS *Tynwald* at Dunkirk, and later SS *Lady of Mann* on D-Day. (Courtesy of Junemary Moyle)

SS *Lady of Mann*, pictured on war service in the Faroe Islands, prior to D-Day. (Author's Collection)

SS *Victoria*, badly damaged by a mine in Liverpool Bay, and later present on D-Day. (Author's Collection)

SS *Ben-My-Chree*, seen in pre-war days. She would carry the US Rangers on D-Day. (Author's Collection)

Eric Cain, the young galley-hand who took part in the D-Day landings aboard SS *Ben-My-Chree*. Like most of the Merchant Navy crew he was trained to assist on the anti-aircraft guns. (Courtesy of Sarah Clucas)

SS *Manx Maid*, after a period of service in the Royal Navy as HMS *Bruce* she returned to Steam Packet passenger service in March 1945. (Author's Collection)

unlawful exportation. Mr. Fernehough, prosecuting for the Customs, said that at ten minutes before midnight on October 15th, two Police Officers, Insp. Wilkinson and Sergt. Steel, were concealed in a passage way at the end of Snargate St., looking out for something entirely different, when they saw defendants approaching from the direction of the town, each carrying a large carton. Insp. Wilkinson stopped them and asked what they were carrying, and defendants replied that they were taking the packages down the street for a stranger they had met, who had arranged to meet them at the end of Snargate St. The cartons were found to contain 48 lbs of cocoa in quarter-pound packets, each marked 5 1/2d. Sergt. Steel accompanied one of the men to the end of the street in the hope of seeing the man who had promised to turn up to collect his cocoa, but no one was there. Hartle, in evidence, repeated the story of the man who had handed them the cocoa outside the 'Eagle' Hotel, shortly after ten o'clock, and said that both he and Cottage had been to several public houses and were 'pretty well merry' at the time. Edward Brown, of Birkenhead, giving evidence on defendant's behalf that he and his fiance saw defendants in the 'Eagle' a little before ten on the night in question, and when he came out, saw them talking outside to a man who had two large cartons. Police Inspector Wilkinson said Hartle appeared at Dover, in December, 1945, on a similar charge when he was fined £10 and one guinea costs.

The Bench imposed a fine of £10 and one guinea costs on Hartle, and £5 and one guinea costs on Cottage, two months and one month respectively.[3]

She never returned to summer passenger duties with the Steam Packet, and being no longer fit for purpose, together with being surplus to requirements following the commissioning of the 'six sisters', the company's post-war replacement steamers, she was laid up in Barrow-in-Furness in February 1949 and scrapped in August at Preston.

Manx Maid had started life as the *Caesaria*, before running aground in fog in 1923 and becoming almost a total wreck. After salvage she was taken over by the Steam Packet Company and renamed. She spent the early part of the war on Royal Navy service as a fleet messenger vessel (and is even credited with shooting down a Nazi aircraft during this period) but was switched to troop carrying duties until July 1940. In October 1941 *Manx Maid* was renamed HMS *Bruce* by the Royal Navy, and became a 'special duties' vessel, under her captain Commander W.S. Moore RN. For much of her Royal Navy service she retained at least a handful of her old Steam Packet crew, including the chief steward, Chief Petty Officer J. Mylrea of Birkenhead who was posted to her on three separate occasions during the war, Petty Officer O.H. Temple of Liverpool, Stoker E. McGinty of Wallasey and Stoker J.E. Kelly of Onchan. At Scapa Flow she went into action with a Junkers Ju 88 aircraft, and after a great battle the little Manx ship shot the enemy into the sea. During the course of her war service she had many trips, and had done all sorts of things for the navy, including crossing some part of the Irish Sea when the weather was so bad that she finished the journey with 8 feet of water in her hold, and her fore screen had been forced back several feet against her bridge. Later she was a target-drawing ship. From the end of March 1942 until March 1945 the Fleet Air Arm used her as a target vessel, and while training was under way for the mission to sink the *Tirpitz*, she played the part of the German battleship. The vessel also transported a number of mysterious crates to the Scottish port of Gourock, widely rumoured to be the Italian crown jewels. She was returned to the Steam Packet on 21 March 1945 and was given a refit (including a new mainmast to replace that which had been removed whilst on Fleet Air Arm service) and put back into full passenger use on the domestic service. She narrowly avoided being destroyed in Liverpool in September 1945 when the Canadian Pacific liner *Empress of Russia*, lying alongside her, caught fire and heeled over. She was another of the old class of ferries due to be replaced by the 'six sisters' and was towed to Barrow-in-Furness for breaking up in November 1950.

At the end of 1940 *Tynwald* was compulsorily purchased by the Admiralty, and was now converted into an auxiliary anti-aircraft ship as HMS *Tynwald*. Six 5.25 inch High Angle guns were fitted to her, and despite having most of her superstructure removed, her displacement was increased to 3,650 tons. Whilst she was refitting in Portsmouth dockyard, a minor irritation for her crew stemmed from the fact that a ship named *Tynedale* was also undergoing repairs, and mail for the two was frequently mixed up. On her early sea trials, she accidentally fired on the tug that was towing the target due to a fault with her fire directing equipment, but this was soon rectified. On her first trip she took a route around Land's End; she was attacked here by German aircraft but successfully drove them off. She travelled up to Tobermory to undertake anti-submarine trials, before entering Belfast Lough. After a year on convoy escort duties around the British coast, in November 1941, she was deployed on similar coastal escort duties in the Western Approaches. Her first commander in Royal Navy service was Captain Frederick Thornton Peters DSO, a Canadian. He was an experienced anti-submarine officer with First World War medal ribbons on his monkey jacket; the ship was loaded with depth charges, and Peters had devised his own method of re-loading the dischargers faster.

On 5 November 1942, now under the command of Captain Philip George Wodehouse, a cousin of the famous author P.G. Wodehouse, she left Gibraltar to join an assault convoy the following day, forming part of the naval force supporting Operation Torch, the North Africa landings. By 8 November, HMS *Tynwald* had arrived off Algiers C beachhead, where for four solid days she provided anti-aircraft support to the transport ships involved in the landings, as well as operating as a radar guard ship directing aircraft from the carrier HMS *Avenger*. Two days later, she left for Bougie arriving on 11 November, again to provide anti-aircraft support, this time directing aircraft from the carrier HMS *Argus*. The following day, while standing by the monitor HMS *Roberts* in Bougie Bay, 100 miles to the east of Algiers, the *Tynwald* was hit on the starboard side after two torpedoes were fired by the Italian submarine *Argo* in the early hours of 12 November. She went down by the bow which became grounded, enabling the rescue of survivors by the *Roberts* and the corvette *Samphire*. Tragically, ten men on board the *Tynwald* were killed. *Tynwald* was now the fourth Steam Packet vessel to be lost to enemy action in the course of the war, and by a bitter irony three of these were the last to be delivered to the company before the outbreak of hostilities. One of her Royal Navy crewmen was Ron Hassall, an able seaman, of Borrowash, Derbyshire. He recalled the incident:

> We were just preparing for the dawn attack when we were hit. It was just 'wuff-wuff' and the ship went over on its side straight away. We abandoned ship immediately and the planes came down to bomb and machine gun us. The lifeboats were smashed up in the explosion, but we saved some of the rafts. I was swimming about in the water for about two hours as far as I know, but you lose all sense of time when the machine gun bullets are about. After we had survived bombs and bullets for about two hours a corvette came and picked us up. We were all in one piece, and only 24 were killed when the torpedo hit the ship. We were landed in Bougie, covered in oil, hungry and with very few clothes on. Planes renewed their attacks, but eventually we were taken off

by destroyer and given baths, khaki shorts, pumps, and a good meal. The journey home was a pleasant cruise. We stopped at Gibraltar, and I had the best meal I had had for weeks – bananas, grapes 1lb for a shilling, apples, oranges and pomegranates.[4]

Another crewman who survived was Chief Petty Officer A.E. May, of 11 St Andrew's Road, Hanwell, for whom it was the fourth time of being torpedoed or sunk in war. In the last conflict, while in the merchant service, he was torpedoed twice and his ship was sunk by shell-fire once. He spent over two years as a prisoner in Germany as a result. Chief Petty Officer May was down below at the time the *Tynwald* went down and the immediate inrush of water swept him off his feet. He scrambled up the iron ladder and when he reached the deck the order was given to abandon ship. After he had been in the oily water for hour, he was taken another vessel. During the whole time he was on board this ship was being dive-bombed. There were many near misses, but the Germans failed to hit it. Eventually he was landed in North Africa with other survivors and told to make his way to another ship. The area was continually being bombed while he was on land, but once aboard ship again he returned to England.

The navigating officer, Lieutenant Edwin Pullan RNR was also wounded. His day job was with the Blue Funnel line, but his RNR training had been on submarines. With the outbreak of war he had been called up to the navy. After twelve months of service back in submarines with HMS *Severn*, he had been appointed to the light cruiser HMS *Dragon* in which he was severely wounded in the Dakar engagement. On recovery he was posted to HMS *Tynwald*, only to be hit again. He was subsequently lent to the Royal Indian Navy, and ended his career as port meteorological officer at Liverpool.

Sub-Lieutenant Engineer Harry Crawley, of Port St Mary, was the only Manxman aboard HMS *Tynwald* when the vessel was sunk that day; he had been a Merchant Navy engineer aboard the ship at Dunkirk, and had transferred to the Royal Navy along with the ship. He remembered many years later that when *Tynwald* was taken into the navy, he had the option to stay with her, and chose to do so because he wanted to serve aboard a ship that was properly armed and able to hit back against the enemy. He had had enough of serving aboard poorly armed merchant ships, and signed a form known as T124X that guaranteed he would get the same pay, 42 shillings a week, as a Merchant Navy engineer officer as well as commissioned rank in the RNVR. His account of the sinking (presumably derived from a letter home) was published in the Manx newspapers. Sub-Lieutenant Crawley was in the mess-room prior to taking over duty at the action station when the ship was struck. Two explosions occurred in quick succession, and lights went out. He dashed forward into the alleyway, but could not find the emergency escape. Just then the fourth engineer rushed out of the mess-room and in the darkness knocked him into the ladder, which he ascended in double-quick time.

By this time the *Tynwald* had taken a list of about 45 degrees. The majority of the ship's company (many of whom were unable to swim) got into the Carley floats and the one remaining whaler, the starboard whaler having been smashed to matchwood. Six officers (of whom Sub-Lieutenant Crawley was one) and eighteen ratings decided to remain aboard the *Tynwald* and await the arrival of another whaler. Soundings were taken, and it was found that there were only 7 fathoms of water beneath her, which made them feel quite happy.

Five minutes later, the first flight of enemy bombers to put in an appearance that day concentrated an attack on the other ships in the vicinity. Meanwhile, the *Tynwald* was slowly sinking, and at 9.30 am the twenty-four men were taken aboard a whaler, transferred to a monitor, and put ashore at Bougie. Their ship had settled in the harbour, her funnel and masts just visible above the water. After leaving Bougie, a call was made at Algiers, and from thence the survivors sailed for a north western British port. Sub-Lieutenant Crawley's parents received a wire from him when he reached Britain, reading simply:

Returned safe and sound with the only clothes I stand up in. Everything else gone.[5]

Crawley was not the only member of the engine room staff to remain with the *Tynwald*. Another former Steam Packet crewman who survived the sinking was the chief engineer, now Lieutenant T.H. Vickers, who came from Grange-over-Sands.

He was awaiting a call to go below decks when the torpedo struck. After the explosion he tried to get into the engine room but found it impossible as it was filling with water so rapidly. After he had reported on the bridge to the captain that the engines were out of action, the ship heeled over and he was thrown into the water, being picked up shortly afterwards by a whaler. He had served with the Steam Packet Company for over fifteen years, and prior to that he had served in the navy in the First World War – he was nearly 60 years of age and a grandfather. For many years he was second engineer in the *Viking*, and went to the *Tynwald* when there was a vacancy after Dunkirk. A letter had been received from him saying that he was safe and home on leave, though he had lost all his effects. Speaking after the sinking was announced, Mr W.O. Orford of the company told journalists that:

> The *Tynwald* went down with colours flying. It has played a noble part in the war.[6]

He added that having been taken over by the government entirely, she was lost to them whatever the outcome of her war service, concluding:

> And a great loss she is, for she was the most modern vessel we had.[7]

By and large the work of these auxiliaries, as supplementary cruisers, anti-aircraft ships and target tugs, though often vital, was unglamorous and did not earn the vessels concerned the enduring fame of some of the better-known ships of the Royal Navy. Yet without the assistance of these former civilian ships, Britain would have been far less able to project naval power around the globe, which was so crucial in a war of this scale.

Chapter Four

Keeping the Home Fires Burning

From the initial outbreak of hostilities in 1939, the directors of the Isle of Man Steam Packet Company neglected to acknowledge the fact that there was a war on, and continued to route its services into Liverpool despite the obvious dangers that this represented for its crews and ships. The city was Britain's major transatlantic port and was certain to be a target for both enemy sea and air attacks. It was only after a serious occurrence which could have had disastrous consequences were it not for good fortune, that they took a more prudent position and decided to shift operations to Fleetwood instead. Leaving aside this incident, the company maintained a vital lifeline for the Island for four years of war, and although there were some civil air services operating in and out of Ronaldsway aerodrome, the ships of the Steam Packet Company were the usual mode of transport for civilians, service personnel travelling to and from postings on the Isle of Man, and for those enemy aliens who were interned on the Island. As the danger posed by U-boats in the Irish Sea began to subside, holiday traffic picked up rapidly in the last two years of the war.

In the early part of the war, the Island's link with Liverpool was maintained by the SS *Victoria* and *Rushen Castle*, with

Snaefell as the standby vessel (this ship had been chartered as a cross-channel troopship in 1939, but had been returned to her owners by Easter 1940. She remained in company service until October 1945 when she was sold for breaking up). The *Victoria* and *Rushen Castle* operated the route in opposite directions, so there was only one sailing each way per day (with no sailing at all on Sundays as was the norm in peacetime). Harry Crawley was just beginning his career at this point, and remembered:

> In September 1939 I was 19 ½ years old and had served 3 ½ years of my engineering apprenticeship with the Steam Packet Company. As George Kennaugh (Senior Apprentice) had been sent to join *Mona's Queen* as a junior engineer I approached the Engineer Superintendent, R.B. Moore, to see if there was a place for me on one of the ships in the fleet, his reply was 'I'll let you know.' At the end of September he sent me to the *Rushen Castle* as Third Engineer, as her Third Engineer had left to join *Mona's Isle*. The *Rushen Castle* only carried three engineers and the Chief and Second Engineer had their Chief Engineer's tickets. That posting lasted until Christmas 1939 and in the New Year when *Mona's Isle* was decommissioned (for RN service), her Third Engineer rejoined *Rushen Castle* and I was sent to Barrow-in-Furness to join *Snaefell* – not a job that I looked forward to. On arrival at Barrow in the

'blackout' the Chief Engineer informed me that I had to return to Douglas and I left Barrow in the 'blackout' by the first train to Liverpool and home.[1]

During wartime the weather in the Irish Sea could be as hostile as any enemy. On Saturday, 27 January 1940, the *Rushen Castle* sailed from Liverpool for Douglas at 10.45 am. An easterly gale blew up which made Douglas harbour unapproachable, but the master was sent a message by radio which instructed him to 'Go to the east', namely to Douglas. The message should have read 'Go to the west', or Peel, on the west coast of the Isle of Man. Captain Bridson duly arrived off Douglas, and was then signalled to proceed to Peel. By the time the *Rushen Castle* had arrived off Peel the gale had backed, and berthing here was not possible either. Eventually the steamer did get into Peel – at 10.00 am on Tuesday, 30 January – after being at sea for seventy-one hours. The lieutenant-governor of the Isle of Man – the Earl of Granville – was one of the passengers. Luckily, he was a seafaring man, having formerly served in the Royal Navy, but his comments on this occasion were not recorded for posterity...

From 1940 onwards the Island had been used to hold interned enemy aliens, and for these people the sea crossing to Douglas marked the final stage in their journey into captivity, having usually been held in transit camps in the north-west beforehand. Hotelier and future founder of the Trusthouse-Forte group, Charles Forte, was born in Italy and remembered that after his arrest:

I was taken first to Kempton Park. There were hundreds of us and we slept rough before being shipped to the Isle of Man. I could not sleep in the crowded saloon so I went on deck and curled up on a coil of rope to doze. I was tired, worried, miserable, and I did not have a penny in my pocket to buy myself food or drink on board, though I noticed that some of the other internees had. All my money had been left at the police station.[2]

Nevertheless, the increasing ferocity of the Luftwaffe's attacks on Liverpool and the mouth of the Mersey caused enormous destruction and disruption to services, with bombs dropped on the city by night and mines dropped in the river by day. A fellow Italian, Nikolai Giovannelli, recounted his own terrifying journey into captivity, which began at 11.30 pm on 25 July 1940:

The tramping of feet, the shouting of angry voices and the clanging of train wagons made a cacophony of noise on the Liverpool Landing Stage, especially as three different languages were being used freely. Suddenly above the clamour sounded a weird moaning as the air raid alert overpowered all else. A moment of shocked silence; then came the drone of German 'planes, the roar of ack-ack's and the explosions of bursting bombs. Liverpool riverside became an inferno and the overhead railway shuddered as though about to collapse on our heads ... At last we were all down on the floating stage. The embarkation went on steadily all through the raid. Bombs were dropping ceaselessly all over the docks to right and left of us, but luckily none of them actually hit the stage or the small Manx steamer, which presently cast off and moved quietly away from that inferno of noise and destruction, sailing down the Mersey to the open sea beyond the bar.

The first thing I did when we got under way was to find my bearings on the upper deck, gather a bunch of prisoners near the lifeboats and give them some instruction on how to improve their chances of survival in case of another attack during the crossing ... after about five hours the faint outline of the Manx coastline could be seen ... We berthed at Douglas at six o'clock in the morning of July 26th ... what a contrast was that peaceful scene to the chaos we had left behind at Liverpool![3]

In July 1940 the *Tynwald*, temporarily back on passenger duties, transferred 1,200 internees from Douglas to Glasgow, for onward transport to Canada. The *Ben-My-Chree*, after repair of the damage sustained at Dunkirk, was also used on these duties in August 1940, when she carried 250 released internees back to Liverpool. The following day, according to sailing sheets, she brought from Liverpool 520 men, mainly Italians bound for the newly opened Peveril Camp at Peel. However, this vessel later returned to troop carrying duties, and the *Victoria* carried many more of those interned, until she too was requisitioned for troopship duties later in the war.

Manx schoolboy Dollin Kelly and his brother were returning home from their public school at Christmas 1940, but arrived at the pier head only to find that sailings were suspended whilst the Royal Navy attempted to clear Liverpool Bay of mines. A gruff Steam Packet deck hand at the bottom of the gang plank told them to come back the next day, but the situation continued as repeated attacks paralysed the city and docks. On the Friday evening, after nearly a week of interruption to vital supplies of mails, newspapers and other goods destined for the Island, shipping agents tentatively informed the Kelly brothers that the ship would sail at 7.00 pm that night. Dollin continues:

> ... When the boat did finally sail ... It was absolutely crammed with people. Soldiers, sailors, airmen, men on their own, women on their own, families with babes in arms and everyone of us looking worn out as we crammed together wherever we could find somewhere to stand. I don't even remember where [my brother] was for most of the journey. The crowd's momentum had propelled me down into the aft well-deck where I recollect being ring-fenced by three of four chaps in khaki when, suddenly, not ten minutes after departing the pier, there was a tremendous crash, the boat shook, then shivered and the already 'blacked out' lights of wartime went out, then on, then out again – exactly like film makers were later to

portray such scenes in the multitude of war films which are still shown on our TVs today. The women hadn't stopped screaming before two more enormous explosions – in very quick succession – rocked the boat but, mercifully, the lights came on within a matter of seconds and, slowly, following a good few relieved exhalations of stifled breath, conversation was resumed and shortly after, normal behaviour as the realisation dawned that we didn't seem to be sinking, and, in fact, the *Victoria* was steaming on without so much as a pause.[4]

The explosions probably came from acoustic mines, which were detonated not by contact but by the vibrations caused in the water by the noise of the ship's engines. The noisy *Victoria*, with its three propellers churning the water, had probably detonated them prematurely and so avoided damage. She was able to make the return trip to Liverpool the next day, however a week later on 27 December 1940 whilst outward bound to Douglas, about 8 miles north-west of the Bar Lightship, she encountered another mine and this time was severely disabled. Fortunately, the weather was calm, and she stayed afloat. The pilot cutter, as well as HMS *Evadne* and the trawler *Michael Griffiths*, came to her assistance and all 200 passengers were saved. The *Victoria* was then towed back to the Mersey by the trawlers *Doon* and *Hornbeam*, and the captain grounded her on Wallasey beach. F.D. Nickson was aboard during this incident, as a child being evacuated to the Isle of Man, and wrote later:

I do not recall any passengers being taken on board the Pilot Boat, which would have been the obvious choice. I seem to remember that the Royal Mail was taken onto the Pilot Boat for safe-keeping (a fact which perhaps may speak for itself, and reflect the attitude of Authority in those less-than-democratic days!). We had an on-deck cabin, so when the explosion took place we were not long in getting outside, where we were taken onto the '*Michael Griffiths*'. Conditions were very much cramped, especially as there was only one 'head' (toilet). Perhaps the number mentioned earlier, 40, was the number taken onto the trawler. Anyway, it seems that we eventually reached Douglas, where it is said that buses were laid on for passengers.[5]

The *Victoria* was repaired at Birkenhead and returned briefly to passenger duties, though sometime later she was to be taken by the Admiralty to become a target towing vessel in the Firth of Forth, before conversion to a troopship. After this the company announced in the press that Liverpool services would be suspended, and the main port for the Isle of Man would now be Fleetwood. As it happened the naval authorities were preparing to close the port to all non-essential transport anyway, as it became the main operations centre for control of North Atlantic shipping. The directors of the Steam Packet Company were gracious enough to confirm that return tickets from Liverpool would be honoured on the Fleetwood route!

Sometime later, Herbert Eisner and a group of fifty other internees travelled by train from Yorkshire not knowing their destination, only that they were headed in a westerly direction. Finally they arrived at Fleetwood, which, a geography lecturer among them noted, had no deep water harbour, so their destination could not be Australia or Canada as some had feared, but must instead be the Isle of Man. Eisner recalled:

> We were instructed to stay in our carriage until all the other passengers had got off the train. It was the first time some of us had seen the Irish Sea glistening in the sun. At low tide you couldn't tell where the beach ended and the sea began.
>
> 'Ere, mate, take hold of this', said one of the soldiers, handing me his rifle. I nearly let go of it.
>
> 'Steady mate, steady,' he said, digging in his pockets for Woodbines and matches.
>
> 'Ta', he winked at me when he had lit his cigarette and retrieved his rifle, 'Court Martial offence!'
>
> I almost felt honoured.
>
> 'There'll be grub on t'boat', he told me. The 'boat', the *Victoria*, one of the Isle of Man Steam Packet Company's, was waiting at the jetty winnowing black

smoke. We dragged our suitcases up the gangway in the hot afternoon sun, watched intently by the other passengers, all male, all wrapped in winter coats, crowding the decks. We stumbled aboard, greeted by the familiar smell of hot engine oil, tea and vomit, suffused here by the extraneous odour of smoked fish. Someone handed us life jackets: no doubt a lesson learned from the *Arandora Star* disaster. Told to put them on we simply hung them round our necks; it was too hot to tie them in position.

Instinct made us go for the boat deck, most of which had already been claimed by earlier arrivals.

'Plenty of room below!' a voice bellowed over the tannoy, but nobody moved.

'Any more for the Skylark!' came the inevitable cockney. Not all of us were recent refugees; when Hitler was still an unknown rabble-rouser, some had come to England as small children, with parents that had found jobs and never bothered to acquire British citizenship.

The ship in wartime was a far cry from her days as a tourist tripper:

Victoria's decks were littered with crude life rafts: empty oil drums, welded together and laced with ropes to hang on to. We squatted in the sun, and consumed our two rounds of sliced bread filled with bacon rashers, which together with a mug of tea, collected at a hatch in the dining salon, made an acceptable lunch for the unorthodox majority of us. Screeching gulls scanned our backwash in the hope of leftovers. The strong wind made our overcoats almost bearable.[6]

As Snaefell mountain and the hotels of Douglas seafront came into view, the Bofors anti-aircraft gunners were rudely awakened from their sleep by a sharp blast on the ship's siren. After disembarking, the internees were led away from the harbour in a crocodile flanked on either side by soldiers with bayonets. Not every party however was as peaceable and well behaved as that of Eisner. On 13 May 1941 a boatload of prisoners from the British Union of Fascists arrived in Douglas, aboard the *Lady of Mann*. Also among them was Hector Emanuelli, who though not a BUF member was British-born of Italian descent. He had spent some time in Italy learning the language, and so the authorities regarded him as also possibly a supporter of fascism as well. Word had already spread on the Island that a ship full of dangerous Nazi sympathisers was due to arrive, and a hostile crowd had gathered in anticipation. Emanuelli recalled that the vessel was met by boos and shouts from the quayside as it docked. The situation was enflamed however by the British Union members, who cheered and called back provocatively. They had also chalked up a slogan on the ship's superstructure:

'MOSLEY FOR PEACE.' The situation looked like it might get out of hand so the authorities decided to keep the prisoners on board overnight, until things had calmed down. They were eventually disembarked at 6.00 am the following day, and then marched to the railway station bound for Peel where they were to be held.

During the Second World War the Isle of Man became quite literally an armed camp, as the authorities realised that its ample hotel accommodation also made it well suited as a training centre. Bases were established for the reception of naval and RAF recruits, as well as two Officer Cadet Training Units (OCTU). For the servicemen undergoing training, the ships of the Steam Packet fleet were the usual method by which they reached the Island or returned home, and many thousands must have travelled this way during the course of the war. One such trainee, Edward Winter Anstey was a cadet with 166 OCTU which was stationed in the Villiers Hotel, on Douglas Promenade. At the successful conclusion of his training, in April 1941, he boarded a steamer for the journey away to commence his active service; he was also leaving behind a wartime romance, and wrote in his diary of the crossing aboard the *Rushen Castle*:

> Grafton, Atkins, Romney & Burrough of B Coy were there to bid us farewell. Major Steer, Hussey & Cole-Hamilton travelled with us on leave. We drew away about 0910 singing 'Kiss Me Goodnight' as Linham followed us along. What a fine CSM he was. Personally

my feelings were too mixed to allow me to remain on deck with equanimity and I speedily joined the gang in the steerage bar where we sang lusty songs & drank immense quantities of 'Blue Label' with Sgt Morgan, also proceeding on leave. We made Fleetwood at 1315 after an extraordinary backward navigation down the channel.[7]

This ship had joined the fleet in 1923, when the Isle of Man Steam Packet Company had taken over the service between Heysham and Douglas, which had been established in 1903. Built in 1898 at Barrow, the *Duke of Cornwall*, as she was known in those days had originally plied between Fleetwood and Belfast operating a joint service for the old Lancashire and Yorkshire and London North Western Railway companies, prior to the Grouping Act. Later she was taken on by the London, Midland and Scottish Railway Company (LMS). When the company acquired the route, they at the same time bought the *Duke of Cornwall* from the LMS Railway, and re-christened her the *Rushen Castle*. (They bought the *Antrim*, renamed the *Ramsey Town*, at the same time but she was withdrawn and scrapped before the war.) A twin screw reciprocating type of vessel, she was 321 feet long with a 37 foot beam, gross tonnage of 1,724 and 4,000 indicated horse power. Though not so powerfully built nor so modern as her more recent colleagues, she was reliable and capable of 17.5 knots per hour. A feature of her construction was the ornate woodwork and carving, in the dining room in particular, which holiday passengers often admired. For most of the war the Island's lifeline was maintained by the *Rushen Castle,* and over the course of those years she carried hundreds of thousands of servicemen, and to many Manxmen who travelled on her during their war service, she brought a breath of the homeland. Laurie Kissack remembered arriving at Fleetwood in January 1943:

> I was in the Manx Regiment and we had been granted three weeks leave – we had not been on leave for three years. We made our way to Fleetwood to catch the Manx boat home and when we arrived at the landing stage there were crowds already waiting to board. Standing at the top of the gangway was the Master, Captain Bridson. He looked down on everyone waiting to board the ship and he addressed the crowd: 'Ladies and gentlemen, if you look around you will see soldiers. They are members of the Manx Regiment and they have not been home to see their loved ones for three years. Please make way for them to board the ship first.' Everyone cheered and stood aside for us to board.[8]

At the time of her eventual disposal she was the oldest boat in the service of the Isle of Man Steam Packet Company. She was however also described as the best by far sea boat in the fleet, and the passing of this comfortable old dog of the sea was regretted by many who had sailed aboard her.

It is perhaps surprising how much the threat of U-boats and mines had receded, and how much the Isle of Man's holiday trade had returned, even before the war had ended; so much so that at times the two vessels serving the domestic route simply could not cope. In July 1943 it was noted that in the previous week-end the number of holidaymakers who failed to get accommodation on the steamer coming to the Island was the highest so far recorded during the war, and this had led to some disorderly scenes. On the Friday 850 people were disappointed, and on the Saturday 800. English newspapers gave the Friday number as 1,200, and stated that between 500 and 600 were in the queue on the Friday night, and referring to the 1,200 turned away on Friday, it was added:

> After threats by those in the queue to rush the station and the steamer, the station was closed, and the police called to assist the railway police. Most of the holidaymakers were from Lancashire and Yorkshire.[9]

Mr A.E. Teare, the assistant manager of the Isle of Man Steam Packet Company, who was present, disputed this report and stated that when the people were told there was no accommodation they dispersed quietly, and there was no threat to rush the station. The newspaper reports indicated, however, that the trouble with the police occurred in the afternoon. On Saturday morning and on Monday the outgoing steamer took all homeward-bound passengers from the Island, though many had arrived early at the pier to ensure that they got aboard.

Wartime bureaucracy and security measures however added greatly to the inconvenience that holiday makers suffered whilst travelling to the Isle of Man. It took the police three-quarters of an hour on 24 July to deal with the 'card filling humbug' required of passengers on arrival at Douglas, and there was some cursing at the Island's ponderous methods. There were about six Manx policemen available to meet the boat, most of them being seriously overworked. The problems with sailing capacity continued that summer however, and on one occasion every national paper in Britain carried articles depicting the scenes of disgruntled holidaymakers, and calls for government action. The mayor of Fleetwood had protested to the Minister of Transport in Whitehall, and Lord Derby had also offered to help, but little could be done to alleviate the situation whilst there was still a military requirement for shipping capacity. Extraordinary reports began to circulate on the Island with regard to the number of people who were planning to endeavour to cross on the August Bank Holiday weekend. These were not the only difficulties faced by summer trippers however – that year two young men found themselves before the courts after police caught them innocently photographing Douglas Harbour and landing piers. Military restrictions were still in place, and this was prohibited, though in court the young men pointed out that many postcards on sale in the shops showed a similar scene.

The same situation with lack of capacity appertained the following summer, and on 1 September 1944 it was reported that in view of the fact that some 600 to 700 people were left behind at Douglas on the previous Saturday, the Isle of Man Steam Packet Company had made arrangements on Sunday for a steamer to sail from Fleetwood light, and this and the ordinary sailing took place on Monday morning. All passengers who wished to travel were thus carried. Although there were some hundreds of people in the queue when the *Snaefell* left Fleetwood, they were not embarked. They could not be carried because the time of sailing was unknown, and it was considered impossible to land them in Douglas in the darkness and with no buses or trains and no accommodation available.

The ongoing annoyance to which passengers to the Isle of Man were subjected, by the examination of their identity documents and travel cards, was mentioned by Mr Samuel Norris MLC at a sitting of Tynwald on 27 June 1944. He said that he was on the pier the previous week, after the steamer had arrived, and passengers were kept an hour before they got ashore. Those for Ramsey had missed their trains as a result. Mr Norris exclaimed:

> I think it is too ridiculous for anything. They begin to examine the cards and to issue permits when the boat is arriving, and that work should be done while the people are still at sea. They go through something similar when they start, and when they reach Douglas it is repeated, over and over again.[10]

In response, Deemster Cowley stated that the War Committee agreed with everything that had been said about this nuisance, and had made representations to the Home Office week by week. The lieutenant-governor added that the War Committee was doing its best, but he had to point out that some of the difficulty arose through the fact that the Conscription (No. 2) Act had not been passed in the Isle of Man, meaning that potential evaders of military service might have been tempted to flee to the Island. Norris in turn responded by pointing out that hundreds of people were affected by these checks, who would have been quite clearly outside of the parameters of the Conscriptions Acts.

As well as the passenger vessels, the company also operated three cargo vessels in the Irish Sea throughout the war. These included the *Peveril*, launched in 1929 and built for the firm by Cammell Laird at Birkenhead, and the *Cushag*, built as the *Ardnagrena* in 1908, and purchased in 1920; as she was a single screw coaster she was small enough to enter the harbours of Peel, Port St Mary, Castletown and Laxey. She carried cargoes to these places, as well as to Douglas and Ramsey. However the service to Peel was suspended by the company in September 1939. It was reported that:

> ... a meeting was held to discuss the matter, when several tradesmen attended on the invitation of the Peel Grocers' Association. Mr J.S. Quirk presided. The question was fully discussed, and the meeting

fully recognised that the Peel trades would not wish the seamen on the cargo steamers to be exposed to any more risks under the present conditions, and under the circumstances they would not approach the Steam Packet Company for a continuance of the steamer to Peel. It was finally decided that a deputation be appointed to join with the Castletown traders to meet the Steam Packet Company on the question of through charges to Peel via Douglas.[11]

She was still serving Ramsey in December 1942, as it was reported that one of the crew George Stewart Kelly, recorded as an able seaman had a £1 note stolen from his wallet whilst the vessel was in the harbour, discharging coal. However it appears that she was sold in February the following year, to a company in Kirkwall, Orkney. The last of the three was the *Conister*, purchased in 1933 (but built in 1921 at Hull). She was frequently seen in Ramsey, unloading goods from Liverpool, before going on to Douglas. In Liverpool on 27 October 1940 she was severely damaged by a bomb during an enemy air attack. She was evidently repaired however, for in July 1945 she was involved an industrial dispute in Douglas. The men employed to unload two coal boats which had arrived in the harbour went on strike, and German prisoners of war were used to unload the coal instead. Steam Packet labourers employed to unload the *Conister* then walked out in protest at the use of German prisoners to break the strike. The dispute was later resolved by the Joint Industrial Council.

Thus the 'Island's Lifeline' continued to operate throughout the long years of war, despite the difficulties and inconveniences that the situation imposed. With the best ships away on war duties, it fell to sometimes elderly and less well equipped vessels to carry on the vital (and at times dangerous) connection with the ports of the Lancashire coast, until such time as peace returned.

Chapter Five

1944 – Operation Overlord

The *Lady of Mann* and *Ben-My-Chree* had spent the years after Dunkirk conveying troops to and from vital destinations, as Britain tried to ensure that the Germans did not establish a foothold on any territory which might serve as a launchpad for invasion, or from which to harass Allied shipping. One such place was the strategically important Faroe Islands in the North Atlantic, where a British garrison was maintained. As early as 1942 however, the troops here were thinking about the inevitable invasion of occupied Europe which was to come. The *Lady of Mann* eventually returned to the Faroes to collect the Lovat Scouts, which would play a key role in that invasion. It was an extraordinary scene when she arrived, and carried away not just soldiers but local sweethearts as well, as recounted by the regimental historian:

> At long last, in May 1942, news came that they were to be relieved by the 12th battalion of that fine Lowland regiment, the Cameronians. The Scouts had repeatedly been told they had done a good job, but they were desperately anxious to get back to the U.K. to join the huge British force of twenty-two Infantry Divisions

and six Armoured Divisions, which had already been training at home for nearly two years, in preparation for final victory. The Cameronians' advance party arrived on 28th May and the Scouts sent theirs by return. At 11.15 hrs on 10th June, the *Lady of Mann*, escorted by H.M.S. *Chiddingfold*, arrived at Thorshavn. To minimise the risk of air attack, a rapid change-over was required. The Cameronians disembarked and trans-shipped for seventeen different destinations with the right baggage, and the Scouts immediately embarked with all their stores, the whole operation being successfully carried out in a few hours under direction of the recently-appointed new Adjutant, Captain W.S. Gammell and Lieut. Bob Ogg. At 22.45 hrs, on a beautiful summer's evening with thousands of Faroese waving goodbye and the Pipers playing 'Happy We Have Been Together', the troopship backed out into Nolso fjord with hoots from all ships, great and small, and set off at full speed for Invergordon. Several Faroe girls, who had married Scouts, travelled bravely with them, but there were some broken hearts among those who waved farewell, whether from the shore or from the ship.[1]

In the summer of 1943, the *Lady of Mann* was also earmarked to take part in the invasion and was sent to Liverpool to be refitted to carry assault landing craft. Will Lister, the purser who had been aboard the *Tynwald* at Dunkirk had joined her at Barrow the previous spring. He remembered that the crew had a fairly shrewd inkling of what the purpose of this refit was. After this, the ship went to the Moray Firth in Scotland, where troops carried out practice landings from her. By now, momentum was gathering for the greatest amphibious operation ever attempted in the history of warfare – the Allied invasion of France, and the opening up of the so called 'Second Front'. Manx people had an early foretaste of what was happening, as some of the convoys which would take part in the landings formed up off the Isle of Man, and indeed some of the landing craft waited in Douglas Harbour for other ships to arrive. Just as they had done at Dunkirk, the vessels of the Isle of Man Steam Packet Company would play a key role in the coming landings. However, one of the ships, SS *Viking* which was moored in the Thames estuary almost did not make it; she had a number of near misses from Hitler's V1 rockets which were becoming an increasing problem in southern England at the time. Captain Jack Holkham remembered later:

> When we went to the Thames to take part in D-day, while at anchor the *Viking* had a very narrow escape. A flying bomb dropped about 90 feet away causing extensive damage. The same thing happened while we were in dock for repairs. Finally she undertook the job of carrying troops to the Normandy beaches, which was a picnic compared to what we had had to put up with during the flying bombs.[2]

At this time, Douglas-born Eric Cain was a 17-year-old Merchant Navy sailor, recently passed out from the training ship *Vindicatrix* as a galley hand. He went into the Merchant Navy 'pool', and was posted to his first ship in Liverpool. This lasted only two days however before she hit an obstruction. His next posting was to an unnamed ship at Gourock on the Clyde. Upon arrival at the port he was surprised to find his new vessel was the *Ben-My-Chree*, recently released from duty as a troopship taking men to the strategically important Shetland Islands and back. At that time, something like 70 per cent of the crew were Manx with a smattering of English sailors, mainly from Liverpool. As well as having the advantage of being surrounded by familiar names, the situation also had its disadvantages. The second steward lived around the corner from Cain in Douglas, and told him to behave himself or he would soon tell his mother! The first trip he made was to South Shields for the ship to be modified for D-Day:

> We came out of the Clyde and there was a really top gale going on ... We had to carry on, to go right up round the top of Scotland, and coming back down through the Pentlands we took a wave on the back end which took the entire back railings off and smashed the back open ... Just one wave that went through. I remember standing where the galley was at the bottom of the staircase and seeing this complete block of water coming down the stairs and going right up into the big restaurant and it

smashed everything up ... We had to keep going, and we called into a small port and lay there about twenty-four hours, then the weather abated a bit and carried on to South Shields. The weather had already done half of what they were about to do in South Shields. They didn't need to strip the outer rail, it had been done! This was when they were going to convert it, for carrying landing barges. They were going to take off all the lifeboats and build it up to take six landing craft, the davits, but we didn't pick the barges up till we got down south...[3]

The ship was also heavily protected with defensive armaments, and even a technically civilian merchant sailor like Cain was expected to leave the galley and assist in the defence of the ship, if she was attacked from the air:

She had a double Oerlikon on each quarter, she had four of those double Oerlikons. After the funnel she had a Bofors manned by army gunners, and the Oerlikons were manned by Navy gunners. We were loaders, you were asked to load them. We never ever got round to banging them off properly, but you were trained on it, you took your part in it, in case someone got hurt, and there was an attack, you took your part in it ... They had onboard two tramlines welded together and you put a rocket in the middle of it and fired it, and it was attached to a reel of very thin piano wire. The idea was that the rocket went up, pulled the roll of piano wire up, and then when it opened up a small parachute came out and held it long enough that it slowly sank back down. The idea was that if any aircraft came along it would snag on the wings. So we decided to try it out but it didn't work, it came back down on the deck and got tangled up![4]

Although the ship was preparing for D-Day, the details of the Normandy landings were a well-kept secret; the only clue as to the *Ben-My-Chree's* destination came from the fact that rather than practicing landing troops on beaches, they repeatedly landed parties of US Rangers in barges against sheer cliffs, which the soldiers scaled with ladders. The reason for this became clear on D-Day itself, when the *Ben-My-Chree* landed troops at Pointe du Hoc, between Utah and Omaha beaches. Two days day before this happened however there was an altercation on board between several of the Rangers' officers – the commander of Able Company, Major Cleveland Lytle, convinced that the mission was suicidal, was drunk in the ship's bar. He was celebrating his recent promotion, but more alcohol than was perhaps wise was consumed. As the evening wore on, he revealed that he had heard rumours that the French Resistance had passed information to the effect that the guns had not yet been installed at Pointe du Hoc, and that the battery was not operational. He was declaring loudly to other officers that they were going to almost certain death in a mission that was pointless. The medical officer of the

Ranger regiment, Captain Walter Block tried to intervene but Lytle punched him, a transgression which fellow officer Len Lomell judged as 'tantamount to beating up your mother.'[5] At this point other officers joined in to restrain Lytle, and he was taken to his cabin where he was detained by order of the ship's captain, Radcliffe Duggan. Upon learning of the incident, the battalion commander had him removed from the ship and detained by military police. Cain however appears to have been unaware of this. Next we find him on D-Day itself:

> We were about ten miles off shore ... the weather was rough. They announced at the time that if we couldn't get the barges down and in the water, they would put the ship ashore. The entire ship was going to go ashore, and we would have to fend for ourselves. This came over the tannoy, from the captain, Duggan ... The first barge we put down didn't have any soldiers in, they put it down to see if it could take the waves, because if it didn't they would put the entire ship ashore. Whether it would have survived getting through the mines we didn't know, because there were a lot of obstructions in the water ... It was very well organised all round really. There was a big warship alongside us, and she was firing salvo after salvo, and you could hear these one ton shells she was firing, going through the air. They were hissing as they went through the air ... I was on watch on deck and could see all this happening.[6]

Duggan was a skilful captain, and having lowered his barges on the lee side, when the heavy swell prevented him from lowering those on the windward side, he swung the ship around and used it to protect them. The Rangers had become friendly with the Manx crew during the time they had been aboard, often passing on American candy and other luxuries. One in particular gave Cain his address in the Bronx and asked him to look him up if he ever made it to New York. This he did on a transatlantic posting after the war, only to find from the man's distraught mother that his friend had later been killed in Normandy.

There was a lull in the action as the *Ben-My-Chree* lay off the Normandy coast, whilst the crew awaited the return of their assault landing craft. Whilst the captain dozed on the bridge, Second Mate Joe Cubbon of Port St Mary and Third Mate Jim Cannon of Peel found time at last for their shared passion – they stood peacefully in the forecastle, leaning over the side fishing, despite being in the midst of war. A reporter who was given access to the ship during the landings reported on what he observed there:

> Men of the Merchant Navy go out of their way to make troops comfortable in their cramped quarters. They find bunks for as many as possible, quietly entertain army guests to drinks from their own limited supplies, lay extra places for meals in their ship's saloon and turn on their screened radio to satisfy the soldiers' thirst for battle front news.[7]

The reporter met the ship's veteran captain, of whom he wrote:

> Step up to the bridge and meet bluff Captain Radcliffe Duggan, 65 this very day, with a record of 52 years at sea ... Duggan's one ambition has been to sail the *Ben My Chree* into Cherbourg as the first ship to enter a reoccupied French port. Three other D.S.Cs serve under him in the *Ben my Chree*, no mean feat for a little ship of 2,600 tons.[8]

The *Lady of Mann* had carried on with her troop transport duties until she was taken over by the Admiralty and converted into an LSI (H), a landing ship for infantry (hand hoisting) and it was then that she was fitted out with three landing craft on each side of the vessel, which were manned by the Royal Navy. She was also equipped with a 12 pounder gun. Whilst anchored off Portland breakwater some of the crew – former fishermen – obtained permission to take a landing craft out for a run and knowing the area to be a good lobster fishing ground, came back with a number of the crustaceans which were enjoyed by the rest of the crew. A few days before the landings took place the invasion fleet including the *Lady of Mann* was visited and inspected by His Majesty King George VI, to whom the master Captain Tom Woods was presented. The next day the ship's company was issued with service gas masks, capes and other anti-gas equipment; clearly there was a fear that the Germans would resort to chemical warfare as in the First World War. Twenty-four hours later troops began to come aboard, and a VIP party comprising, among others, Prime Minister Winston Churchill, Field Marshal Jan Smuts, and Foreign Secretary Ernest Bevin paid a visit. The official historian of the Canadian Régiment de la Chaudière records:

> Embarkation began on June 1. While 'B' Company took up position on Landing Ship Infantry (LSI) *Monowai*, 'D' Company and the alternate HQ embarked on *Clan Lamont*. The rest of the unit embarked the next day, with 'A' Company going aboard the *Prince David* and 'C' Company and Regimental HQ going aboard the *Lady of Mann*. As for the 'Support' company, it was scattered in various Landing Craft Tanks (LCTs) and Landing Ship Tanks (LSTs). Thus on June 3 almost all the men assigned to Operation NEPTUNE were already on the ships, impatiently awaiting the signal for the departure of the Supreme Allied Commander, General Dwight Eisenhower.[9]

The diary of one of the galley cooks, a Laxey man from South Cape named Bobby Skillicorn, gives a wonderfully evocative picture of daily life on the ship, and is a world away from the dry official accounts. For 4 June 1944 (a Sunday) it reads as follows:

> Service on board. Messages read from Army and Naval chiefs. It's invasion. Weather interferes. Postponed

24 hours ... Tension increases. Feel quite calm myself. My thoughts mainly at home. We are in the first assault. I talk to Eighth Army crack troops on board and tough French Canadians. Vast Armada on the move. Wonderful sight. I think of Doris and the baby I haven't seen in a special way tonight.[10]

Purser Bill Lister remembered that on the night of 5 June, the *Lady of Mann* had embarked troops in the Solent. At about 10.00 pm he went up to the bridge, and came across a young Canadian officer looking out across the hundreds of ships lying shoulder to shoulder in readiness for the operation to come. The man was awestruck by the vast scale of the armada in front of him, but admitted to Lister that he wouldn't have missed it for the world. Lister, perhaps because he had already had first-hand experience of war and the young officer had not, could not sleep that night, there was so much on his mind:

So I decided to go and talk to the men in the engine room. There was so much tension and I wanted to help take their mind off things. After about half an hour we were moving out into the Channel and as I went back up I ran into a sergeant of the Royal Berkshires and suggested having a drink. We shared a glass or two of whisky in my cabin and he told me all about his life, his wife and children. Eventually we said good night, I wished him luck and we went our separate ways. The next day when the operation was well under way I asked after this sergeant from the men in the landing craft. Well, it nearly broke my heart – they told me he had led the dash and was mown down about halfway up the beach. It was terrible – he was such a fine man.[11]

Stanley Shimmin was also a crewman on board, and recalled the ship going into action on D–Day:

We were off the Isle of Wight, where we joined a convoy, and at dusk we set off with our escorts, all in different lanes. We saw a coaster on fire, which must have been full of small arms ammunition, as bullets were going off like mad, and you could see by the light of the shells and bullets, the crew trying to get clear. The captain of the '*Lady*' was keen to go over to see if she could pick up any of the crew, but as he started to move the ship out of line a voice hailed us 'get back on your course, you are not a rescue ship.' it was one of the escort ships, a United States Coastguard cutter that came speeding past and went to help the burning coaster.[12]

Lister meanwhile continued:

We went in to within about six or seven miles off Juno Beach. When we got near, there were midget subs on the ocean floor which had to rise and flash a green light seawards to give us the parameters for the landings. The expedition had to face the German Atlantic wall and there were tremendous fortifications and obstacles everywhere, with barbed wire in between. Hundreds of rounds of ammunition were being poured in – the noise was deafening – but we were well protected by American and British warships and the German subs couldn't get near.[13]

Again and again the landing craft returned to the *Lady* for more troops, proceeding through a haze of smoke and a blizzard of fire, until three of them were put out of commission by enemy action. Skillicorn continues:

Close friend McDonald fatally wounded first by exploding mine then shot by sniper as his coxswain tried to bring him to another craft. Briggs from Preston injures foot. Doctor amputates three toes. We leave for home.[14]

On D-Day she lay 5 or 6 miles off the selected beach, but later was able to come within about a mile. The *Lady* also brought back 200 prisoners. They were a mixed lot, and included Hungarians, Poles and Czechs. One eye witness observed that they seemed very pleased to have been captured. Another member of the ship's company stated that the most striking feature of their five trips to the beaches was the contrast between these 'no-trouble' ventures and those at Dunkirk and other French ports in which the *Lady* played such a magnificent part when evacuating Allied troops in 1940.

Then the ships had little or no protection, and very few arms to beat off air or sea attack. The unnamed crewman had made the acquaintance of some of the Canadian commandoes on the first trip, and had nothing praise for their high morale. He continued:

> Our first load out consisted of Canadian and British commandoes. These are great men, and have put the fear of God into the Germans, according to some of the prisoners we have brought back. One of these prisoners was a German war correspondent who had been sent to France to cover the invasion and the hurling back of the Allied troops into the sea. He told how the German High Command had been deceived by a convoy which apparently was going to land a considerable way up the coast to the north-east. The Germans rushed troops to repel this landing, and the correspondent went with them. When the Allies landed in Normandy, he was rushed back, and arrived just in time to be captured. This man had a lot to say about our Commandoes and their knives, the knives especially.
>
> Our ships had landed so many troops in the first two days that although the four days' hold up by storm was serious, it was by no means disastrous Those landed were not only strong enough to hold on, but extended their holding.

Now we had so much sea and air support, and were so well armed ourselves, that we had perfect confidence we would get there. There was, at times, plenty of gunfire from our escort, and the depth charges shook us up a bit, but we only saw one Jerry plane, and that was shot down just as it turned, probably to attack us. We were the biggest ship in the convoy, and this occurred on our last trip home. The four days when we were anchored off the beaches owing to storm were bad, as we could not transfer our passengers to the landing craft. These craft suffered badly, as their anchors would not hold, and two of them tied up to the *Lady* for two days.[15]

The wounded from the beaches which the *Lady* carried home were made as comfortable as possible. However the captured Germans who were going back to British prisoner of war camps proved to be less popular. On 9 June Skillicorn's diary records:

Embarked 250 Hun prisoners. Refused to assist in preparation of hot meal for them. Wounded American stretcher cases arrive. I assist in getting them aboard and assist dressings. I volunteer after long day to cook a hot meal for wounded, including Germans.

The following day he adds:

Much needed rest. Received tonic, a letter from Doris. Replied cheerfully, but wasn't.[16]

About a month before D-Day a stray cat, which was expecting kittens, had adopted the *Lady* as its home. During the noise and furore of the landings it had gone missing. Lister recalled that:

> Once we had disembarked all the troops, the skipper (Captain Woods) started worrying about the cat. We sent out a search party and discovered her in the lower sleeping quarters. She had given birth to six kittens.[17]

After the third week of crossings the weather became atrocious, and the *Lady* had to lie out in the Seine Bay for four days – the same experience, it was recorded, befell the *Ben-my-Chree* under Captain Duggan. Water for the engines and for meals began to run short, and the crew were sharing their rations with the troops. The gale force winds produced waves 50 feet high, and in the difficult conditions an American landing craft hit the *Lady*, badly damaging the bow and bow rudder. Bobby Skillicorn records:

> Everyone tired out. Some troops seasick. Eerie sight watching all these ships riding out the storm. Pity the poor fellows on ships astern. Unable to get food to them. Made several attempts. Heavy gunfire inshore.[18]

The following day the convoy was still stormbound, and Skillicorn's diary reads:

Enemy air activity increases but so far God is good to us. Mines are our chief danger just now. Too rough for U and E boats. Looks like another night here. Gave my dinner and tea to hungry Americans. A quiet week with Doris would be very nice now, and badly needed.[19]

The hundreds of civilian and landing ships crossed in company with a powerful naval escort including – as was known at the time from official reports – such famous warships as the *Warspite* and *Belfast*, which put up a tremendous barrage. There was such an immense air umbrella that only one enemy aircraft was seen to come close, which was quickly brought down with a burst from one of the escorting warships. It crashed about 100 yards behind the *Lady*. There were shells from the enemy batteries, but very few. The most intense enemy bombardment was on one particular day when for a period one would see a shell about every half-hour. Up to that point the *Lady* had made five crossings, and at least 85 per cent of her crew at this time were Manx, one of these men told a journalist:

It made you feel safe when you saw all those planes ... Everyone aboard reckoned that the minesweepers had done a great job. Without them, the landing would have been impossible. It was marvellous to be able to steam up to the French coast without trouble.[20]

The war correspondent of the *Daily Mail*, Reginald Eason, was allowed access to the Manx ships in the invasion fleet, and mentioned them in a report carried by the *Daily Mail* on 16 June 1944:

> Earlier I went aboard three other famous cross – channel steamers known to millions on the Liverpool – Isle of Man ... routes. All took part in the initial assault and have crossed to Normandy on two or three occasions since. One of them, the '*Victoria,*' commanded by Capt. J.J. Keig of Port St. Mary, Isle of Man, grand old lady of the cross-channel packets, is 37 years old, and in the last war carried one and a half million troops to France without mishap. She took across British Commandos, some of the first troops to land on D-Day, and has also put hundreds of American troops on the beaches. 'The stickiest moment was when a German plane just cleared her mast. I don't know who was most scared – him or us,' said the captain. Another ship. R.M.S. '*Lady of Mann.*' commanded by Capt. T.C. Woods, of Douglas, took hundreds of troops to Bernieres on D-Day, and has made three further trips with larger groups of United States troops.[21]

Towards the end of the month the *Lady* went into dry dock to repair the damage done to her bow, but even then the crew had their rest disturbed by enemy air activity. On 5 July she was back at sea again off Falmouth awaiting orders.

It was Tynwald Day, and so the ship flew the Manx flag in celebration. Bobby Skillicorn added:

Quietest day since the invasion.[22]

The *Victoria*, now fitted out as an LSI (H) had been based at Southampton from the summer of 1943, employed in practising landings for the forthcoming invasion. It was repetitive but vital work, and the high level of training of those involved in the attack was one reason for the high rate of success. On D-Day itself, *Victoria* was one of the vessels scheduled to land troops on the western edge of the bay of Arromanches. Despite the unexpected presence of a German flak ship in the bay which put up heavy resistance, the British troops carried by the *Victoria* were from 47 Royal Marine Commando, part of the 4th Special Service Brigade, and these men were landed successfully. Combined Ops Signals Officer Charles Armstrong remembered:

> I was combined operations signals officer aboard HMS *Princess Josephine Charlotte*, which is classed as a landing ship infantry assault, working mainly with Commandos. The landing craft are carried on davits, port and starboard sides, we carried eight such craft, the SS *Victoria* was to go in with us on D-Day, she carried six LCA, this made up a flotilla of fourteen landing craft, I was boat officer in No. 4 boat.

The classes I had been instructing over the past year were aware we were training hard for a special mission, when we will be put to the test, most of us guessed what it would be. The question was where? The training had been arduous and realistic, there were a few unavoidable casualties.

The boat crews consisted of quite a few veterans, from operations such as Dieppe, North Africa, Anzio etc., it certainly felt good to have men like this around you, quite often I would visit their mess deck with a pipe full of baccy and spend an entertaining hour with them listening to humorous banter and amusing songs. The oldest among them was a character 'Seaweed Sam', a strange but fascinating person who fitted his nickname. There was a good camaraderie among officers and men without any lack of discipline or respect. We loaded No. 47 Royal Marine Commando at Berth 59 in Southampton Docks, on Friday 2nd June 1944. They were an impressive body of men intensely proud of their historical background and keen to get on with the task before them. I felt honoured to be associated with them.[23]

At the time the ship's officers were still mainly Manx, like her master Captain John Keig, but the officers who commanded her landing craft were largely from the RNVR. For some days after this she carried American reinforcements to Utah Beach, where there had been fierce resistance, and afterwards returned to Arromanches carrying troops and supplies for the bridgehead there. When the battlefront moved beyond Normandy in the autumn of 1944 she became an unofficial emergency hospital ship, picking up wounded and taking them back to hospitals at Dieppe. The official history of one American medical unit which she carried reads:

> 11 July 1944, it was time to go, so, clad in fatigues, dressed in impregnated clothing, loaded with individual gear and packs, the 107th Evac Hosp departed England for the continent. Channel crossing would take place aboard a British transport, the SS *Victoria*. The Nurses went into the hold with the other Officers; the EM were set up everywhere else. The voyage itself was uneventful, except conditions which were appalling. The ship proved poorly ventilated, men and women were packed like animals, the sea was rough with many sick notwithstanding anti-seasickness pills, and food (not many felt hunger) was distributed in the form of 10-in-1 rations. Fortunately, the sea voyage was short and around noon 12 July 1944, the French coast was in sight. It was a beautiful and sunny day. After being transferred to the smaller LCTs, everyone moved on to one of the piers, part of the Omaha Beach artificial (Mulberry) harbor complex.[24]

Troopship duties continued through the summer of 1944. In September the ships were back at Ostend, where they had last been in the spring of 1940. One of the men who was carried in to combat at this time was Frank Coutts, who served in the 52nd (Lowland) Division, which expected to go into action by air as part of the Battle of Arnhem. That was not to be, but:

> Now at last we were needed in France as an ordinary, well-trained, Infantry Division. One Brigade (157) was already there at the sharp end in Holland, where the Arnhem operation had ground to a halt. The 4th Bn embarked on the *Lady of Mann* at Southampton on the 16th of October. The Embarkation officer was Arthur Nelson KOSB from Melrose; he had seen the Battalion off to France in 1940. This time we wouldn't be back so soon. We landed at Ostend with some difficulty – unopposed, except by sunken shipping – quite close to the front line because the Germans were still fighting a fierce rearguard action in the Breskens Pocket on the south bank of the Scheldt.[25]

On this same trip Skillicorn set foot on European soil for the first time, for when the *Lady* arrived at Ostend, and disembarked 1,100 soldiers and equipment in just 23 minutes, he got the chance to go ashore and look around. He saw HM King George VI boarding a destroyer, and a *Pathe News* cameraman filming the occasion. He also met local civilians, and added in his diary:

Spoke to many Belgians and gave food and cigs to some. Some looked as if they had had a rough time. Place badly damaged. Two or three Manxmen among the troops, including John Caine, drapers, of Athol Street.[26]

Once again, the sheer carrying capacity of the Isle of Man Steam Packet Company's ships had proved to be a decisive factor in an amphibious operation. They had helped to ensure that the opening of the Second Front in Europe, from the Normandy landings through to the liberation of Belgium and Holland, was achieved successfully. Those ships, with their largely Manx crews, had carried Commandos, Rangers and medics to the invasion beaches, together with stores, ammunition and supplies; British, Canadian and American troops had crossed in their thousands, and wounded, men on leave and prisoners of war had crossed in the opposite direction.

Chapter Six

Epilogue

In the last days of 1944 and into the early weeks of 1945, Hitler made a final bid for victory in the west, using troops that he could ill afford to spare from the Eastern Front. The so-called Battle of the Bulge (or Ardennes Offensive) was intended, in the Führer's deluded mind at any rate, as a repeat of the momentous events of May 1940, only this time with the result of splitting and defeating the British and Americans. It ended in ultimate defeat, but Allied reinforcements were rushed to the front line to shore it up. Manx vessels carried British troops of No. 3 Commando, as Stan Scott remembered:

> At the appointed time, everybody was at Worthing station. Two blokes had turned up drunk, which would not have been a problem, but they also arrived without their kit. They were immediately booted out, their green berets taken away. We travelled to Gravesend, boarded the *Lady of Mann* to Ostend, and finished up in the snow and ice of the Ardennes Forest. The weather was like the Russian Front ...[1]

She was at this point based in the Thames estuary, and the main danger to the *Lady* now came from Hitler's rocket propelled flying bombs, the V1 and V2 which were simply too fast for most conventional fighters to be able to intercept. London was an obvious target, and these weapons often fell within earshot. Bobby Skillicorn recorded in his diary for 4 March 1945:

> Flying Bombs again just after midnight. 3am claxton [*sic*] went again followed by announcements that raid was by bombs. Bombs were dropped further down river. All clear 3.30am. Today wet and cold. Received letter from Doris. Wrote 6.45am and claxton [*sic*] goes again here the system of warning is good. 10am weather good. More ships in convoy than usual minesweepers astern exploded mine we passed over. Shook *Lady* from stem to stern. Lucky do. Burned face and right arm with boiling fat Doctor advised me to take afternoon off. Able to write anyway that's something. More bodies, mostly soldiers, floating in mid-Channel. No sign of distressed ship ... Empire cargo boat strikes mine and is beached.[2]

Tuesday, 8 May 1945 was VE Day. Skillicorn recorded in his diary that all the Manx ships present on trooping duties joined the celebrations:

> All work stops on the *Lady* at once. 11am and orders are received for ship's sirens and bells to commence celebrations. Ship's flags go up and Tilbury docks soon

> change into carnival grounds. The *Viking* flies a huge Manx flag at masthead. *Ben-my-Chree* gets special welcome as she arrives. Clinking of glasses and choirs heard everywhere. Planes do a victory roll overhead.[3]

That evening he went into London and continues his account:

> Saw Royal family on balcony at Whitehall. Wonderful spectacle as flood and searchlights are switched on. Westminster Square becomes huge dance floor as massed bands of Coldstream and Grenadier Guards strike up. Whole place one seething mass of people.[4]

Even though the war in Europe was officially over from 8 May 1945, the Admiralty retained a number of Manx ships for troopship work. The *Ben-My-Chree* carried the first group of 250 British servicemen to be demobilised from the European theatre when she departed Ostend for Dover on 18 June 1945. Practically all of the group wore First World War medal ribbons, and many had also been decorated. As troops returned from Europe, some of them were carrying souvenir firearms prohibited in the UK, despite the efforts of the military police to prevent this. A 19-year-old Royal Navy cook named William Stanley Evans found himself in trouble with Dover magistrates in September of that year, after he twice found such a firearm secreted on the deck of the *Ben*. The first he sold to a Black American GI, the second he was attempting to sell when the police heard of his activities. Magistrates fined the young cook a total of £5 for the misdemeanours. Also among those who departed via Ostend were released prisoners of war, including among them Corporal Vic Gillingham of 527 Company Royal Army Service Corps, who had been captured at St Valéry during the fall of France. It was a remarkable coincidence that he returned home on the *Ben-My-Chree*, for this was also the vessel which had brought him to France in January 1940. The *Ben* was still on this duty in December when she was damaged whilst lying at the Admiralty pier, Dover by the Southern Railway steamer *Invicta*, carrying troops from Calais. The *Invicta* collided with her stern, following a failure of the internal telegraph system.

Other dangers still faced the ships of the Isle of Man Steam Packet Company, even though the war was over. On Christmas Eve 1945 troops going home on leave crossing the Strait of Dover wore life jackets because of the peril to shipping posed by floating mines. As the *Victoria*, now a Channel troopship, was casting off from Calais packed with 1,500 men coming home for Christmas, a warning was given of mines by loudspeaker and each man was ordered to put on a lifebelt. The ship had been held up in harbour since the previous afternoon because of the scourge, which was made especially worse by strong easterly winds whipping up the Channel. The mine peril to shipping was as serious as it had ever been, and the previous days had seen reports coming in hourly of more mines being washed up along the Sussex coast. Captain Harry Kinley, now returned to Steam Packet service after his time as a River Mersey pilot, remembered his own experience at this time, sailing out of the Thames estuary:

> After the war had finished … we were going across, and one of our own mines came loose. The war had finished [and] we were going to Ostend a lot … This particular night, I was Second Mate of the *Lady of Mann*, and I was on watch. We were going across, and Captain Tom Woods, he was down in his cabin, you know, lying with his pipe there. He were a wonderful old chap, and at the wheel was a fellow called Harry Halsall, Port St Mary seaman. Another called Johnny Clewis out on the port wing, and little signalman out on the flying bridge and he was up there and I think I had a Peel man on my starboard watch … and it was blowing about force six or seven, squalling to seven and going down to six and five even. And there was a lot of cloud in the sky, and every now and then there'd be a break in the moon; beautiful moon, but just breaking occasionally. You talk about the Good Lord watching over us, and we all spotted it at the one time. Here, right in the light from the sky, down where the moon break. Here we could see the mine. It was a huge thing … I said to Harry Halsall, 'Harry! For God's Sake hard to starboard.' We were going full speed, and when you go full speed in a ship, she lies over like that you see. 'Hard to starboard!' we said, and the little signalman, he jumped from the

flying bridge, out onto his legs onto the bridge. Clewis was out on the port wing. He came dashing through, and he tripped over the step that the Quarterman was standing on and he fell at my feet. And then we went 'Midships' and 'hard a port', and of course the ship rolled ... and went down on her side ... But Captain Tom Woods he was such a wonderful chap. Because the ship rolled he came up and said, 'What's wrong, Harry, what's wrong?' 'Well sir, I don't think you've got so near to a mine, end on to a mine, and missed it in your life before nor ever will again.' 'Aye, aye, that's right. Good, good look out, yes, yes. All right Harry, you know where I am if you want me'. He was a wonderful fellow. He'd confidence in you...[5]

Manx soldier Laurie Kissack was demobilised from the army in February 1946. He recalled:

The Manx Regiment arrived at Ostend along with hundreds of other troops to board a ship to sail to Dover. To our joy we saw the *Victoria* at the quayside ready to sail and the captain was Captain Bridson. There he was standing at the top of the gangway and once again he addressed the crowd: 'Well boys, I know you are all anxious to board this ship and get home, but please will you make way for the Manx lads to come on first because we are a Manx crew on a Manx boat and these are our boys.' All the other troops laughed and cheered and let us through. When we got on board good berths were found for us and Captain Bridson went around talking to all of us – he seemed to know most of us or someone related to us.[6]

On another occasion tragedy struck when one of the soldiers being carried home by the *Lady of Mann* tripped and fell off the side of the ship. Amazingly his greatcoat became caught and prevented him from falling directly into the sea. Frantic efforts were made to launch one of the ship's lifeboats and get it to him, but he fell into the waves and was lost before it could reach him. It was not until March 1946 that the vessel was released from war duties and returned to the Isle of Man. Before she left Dover a little ceremony took place in that town, which evidenced the popularity of Captain Woods there, when he was presented with a pipe, complete with case and tobacco, and a very artistic illuminated address executed by Mr G.K. Stones, a customs officer. It was headed by a water colour of the barque, *Wytchwood*, a deep-sea jury-rigged vessel in which Captain Woods sailed in 1910, and below this was a water colour of the *Lady of Mann*. The inscription on the address read: 'Presented to Captain T.C. Woods, OBE, to commemorate 53 years sea service and an appreciation of good fellowship by the staff of His Majesty's Customs, Dover.' It also gave details of the main epics of the *Lady of Mann*'s war-time career: 'Evacuation of Dunkirk, five trips.' 'Evacuation of Le Havre.' 'Evacuation of Cherbourg.' 'Evacuation of Brest.' 'Evacuation of La Pallice.' 'D-Day operations.' 'Transport of approximately two million troops.' 'Let the Hurricane Roar.' The latter phrase was the motto used by the sea-faring men of the Dover patrol, to whom the *Lady* had become a familiar sight.

Shortly afterwards she arrived in Douglas. A war-stained ship with the grim, grey paint peeling from her hull, the signal, 'Well done, *Lady of Mann*, welcome home,' was flown from the pier in international code as she arrived. Audible greetings echoed out over the water as the big ship crept slowly in between the Victoria and Battery piers, and the receiver-general (Mr R.C. Cain MLC JP) spoke over the loud speaker system:

> Captain Woods, officers and men of the *Lady of Mann*, it is a great pleasure for me, the Receiver-General, to welcome you to your home harbour, which you all love so much. Thanks for all you have done for Ellan Vannin.[7]

His words were followed by the strains of 'O Land of Our Birth,' recorded over the loud speaker, and this was the great moment of the welcome as the many men prominent in the public life of the Island, bared their heads as they stood on the upper deck of the pier, in homage to their Island home and in salutation to this fine ship and her gallant crew.

Captain Woods was seen on the bridge directing the mooring of his vessel, and officers and crew stood modestly about the deck with no outward sign of the deep emotion which must have been stirring them within. A poem of welcome, written by Mr G.R. Masheder, and read by Mr G.J.A. Brown, editor of the *Isle of Man Times*, was relayed to the men on board as the vessel was being moored, and a band of the Royal Naval School of Music played lively selections on the pier. Mr A. Robertson OBE JP, chairman of the Steam Packet Company took the microphone and said:

> On the occasion of the arrival of the *Lady of Mann* at her home port, after years of strenuous war service, I tender to you, your officers and crew, on behalf of the directors and management, our congratulations on a sale return, and heartfelt thanks for the splendid services which the *Lady of Mann* and the other vessels of the fleet have rendered in the cause of freedom. We rejoice at the signal honour which His Majesty the King saw fit to bestow on you in the recent Honours List, an honour which we regard not only as a well-merited tribute to yourself personally, but to the gallant band of officers and men who served under you. In conclusion, may I, in the time-honoured phrase, wish God-speed to the *Lady of Mann* and all who sail in her.[8]

Brief words of greeting were also uttered by the mayor of Douglas (Councillor T.C. Cowin JP), who said:

> As Mayor of the Borough, and on behalf of the people of Douglas. I extend to you a most cordial welcome on your return home. You have had a hard and strenuous

time, but we are all delighted that you have come back safe and sound after a period of war service which has been outstanding. Good luck to you all.[9]

Captain Woods smilingly acknowledged the welcome, and in his characteristic way briefly said:

It is a great pleasure to have such a reception on our return, and on behalf of my officers and men I thank you all for coming down to see us.[10]

Two buses then conveyed the skipper and a number of his crew to the town hall for a civic reception. In his speech of welcome, the mayor said:

I deem it a great privilege as first citizen of the Borough, to be able to extend to Capt. Tom Woods and the officers of the *Lady of Mann* a most cordial welcome on their return home. We have heard and read with great admiration of the service they have rendered during the war – service which has been remarkable for the courage and fortitude displayed. I know that Captain Woods had one great ambition, and that was to bring back home his ship after the war had ended. We are extremely delighted that his ambition has been realised, and that he himself has returned unscathed. Captain Woods I know you are a very shy and modest man, and I want to spare your blushes, but I do want you to know

> that the people of this town and this Island are proud of you and the service you have performed for your King and country. That service has already received Royal recognition, and we all congratulate you most warmly on the honour which has been conferred on you. In conclusion, I cannot do better than say to you, your officers and your crew, a very sincere and warm 'Thank you' for your splendid service.[11]

This speech was greeted with warm applause, and the town clerk called upon the captain for a reply. Captain Woods in response said:

> Speech-making is not one of my high spots, but I am delighted with the way we have been received, and on behalf of my officers and men I would like to return very sincere thanks. I would like it if more of the men who went through the mill with me had been here.[12]

He went on to mention some of those men by name – Chief Officer W. Saunders, who was with him in the 1940 evacuations, and had since retired; Chief Officer Bob Clucas, who was in the *Mona's Queen* when she was sunk, and in the *Lady of Mann* on D-Day; John Kerruish, a former second officer; Frank Griffiths, also a former second officer; and Norman Taylor, a former second engineer. They had all done excellent work. He concluded:

This ordeal is worse than encountering mines! Anyway, I am pleased I have been able to bring the '*Lady*' back in one piece.[13]

This was greeted with further applause. Among those of the ship's company who signed the visitors' book at the town hall, and who were on board the *Lady of Mann* throughout the whole period of her war service, were: Mr H. Almond (chief steward), Mr A.V. Garrett (chief engineer), Mr C.H. Kelly, (third engineer), and Mr J. Cooil (chief cook).

The ship left Douglas on the following Sunday morning for Birkenhead, where she was to be refitted at Cammell Laird's for her peace-time job.

In May 1946 the *Ben-My-Chree* was also released from war service, but her duties had taken their toll and she was in poor condition. During her war service a German raider had crashed on her foredeck, and she had sustained severe bow damage. It was necessary for her to enter Morpeth Dock, Birkenhead, for a refit (including a shortened mainmast) before she could return to passenger duties, though this was delayed somewhat by a shipyard strike. The immediate problem faced by the company when the war ended was not simply a question of replacing the lost ships; the difficulty was that among those lost were those newer ships, with greater capacity.

The company's pre-war fleet and tonnage consisted of 13 ships: *Lady of Mann* (3,104); *Ben-My-Chree* (2,586); *Mona's Queen* (2,753); *Tynwald* and *Fenella* (2,376 each);

Manxman (2,030); *Viking* (1,957); *King Orry* (1,877); *Snaefell* (1,713) *Victoria* (1,658); *Mona's Isle* (1,688); *Manx Maid* (1,512); *Rushen Castle* (1,700) the total displacement being 27,330 tons. Four of these ships had been sunk by enemy action. These being *Fenella*, *Tynwald*, *Mona's Queen*, and *King Orry*, which took part in the First World War and led the German fleet to surrender at Scapa. In total they displaced 9,005 tons. A fifth ship, the *Snaefell*, then lying at the Tongue Douglas Harbour, was due to be sold for scrap. These ships together could carry 10,000 people to the Island in a single trip. They were to be replaced, for the time being, by 2 ships which would carry 4,000 between them (the new *King Orry* and *Mona's Queen*, ordered in 1945). The *Manxman*, taken by the Admiralty and renamed *Caduceus*, was shortly to become available again, to join the *Ben*, *Lady* and *Victoria*, which were already released. The company had been particularly anxious to get the big ships, the *Lady of Mann* and *Ben-My-Chree*, which carried about 5,500 passengers between them, back on the service. The *Manx Maid* was being reconditioned in Barrow, but that would not bring the Steam Packet Company's problem to an end. With the two new ships, the fleet which would be at the disposal of the company when all the ships were back on passenger service, could only carry approximately 20,000 people, compared with the 26,000 passenger capacity of the pre-war fleet.

In August 1946 the captain and officers of the Isle of Man Steam Packet Company's vessel, *Victoria*, were presented with a mahogany salver, on which there were three brass shields with appropriate lettering, to commemorate the part played by the ship in the D-Day operations. The donors of the gift were the officers of the landing craft the *Victoria* took to the beaches. The officers of the *Victoria* in turn presented the gift to the company, and the manager, Mr A.E. Teare, accepted it on their behalf from the chief engineer, Mr W.A. Cain. On the centre shield, surmounted by a V for victory, there was an engraving of the ship, with the six landing craft, together with an inscription: 'D-Day 6th June, 1944. Presented as a token of esteem to the captain and officers of the S.S. *Victoria* from officers of 508th L.C.A. Flotilla.'

The left-hand shield bore the names of the deck officers of the ship on D-Day: Capt. J.J. Keig (since deceased); First Officer, J.E. Quirk; Second Officer, R.E. Gelling; Third Officer, A.W. Kissack; Purser, J.E. Kerruish; First Radio Officer, A.V. Davidson; Second Radio Officer, T.D. Jamieson; Chief Steward, J.F. Brown; Carpenter, J.R. Taggart. The right hand shield bore the names of the engineer officers and the medical officer as follows: Chief Engineer, W.A. Cain; Second Engineer, C. Watterson; Third Engineer A.A. Kellie; Fourth Engineer, J. Kneale; Fifth Engineer, J.E. Gelling; Sixth Engineer, F. Murphy; Seventh Engineer, H. Whiting. Medical Officer, Surgeon-Lieutenant H.A. Doyle.

This however did not mark the conclusion of her service, and it was not until March 1947 that the Admiralty released the *Victoria* from government work as a troopship crossing the English Channel. It took a little time for the Island's tourist industry properly to get back on its feet, but the

Steam Packet Company continued to press ahead with the immediate rebuilding programme embarked upon at the end of the war, to replace the ships which had been lost to enemy action. It would be some years before this was achieved, but the new *King Orry* (IV) and *Mona's Queen* (IV) would be joined by four other new ships to complete what were known as the 'six sisters'. Appropriately Captain Oscar Taylor was in command of one of these, the new ship *Tynwald* (V) on her maiden voyage to Douglas on 31 July 1947. He returned to the *Manxman*, however, to take her on her last voyage from Harwich to Barrow. He retired in 1957 and died in 1972 at the age of 79.

On 23 September 1954 at noon the 'Grand Old Lady', the 49-year-old *Viking* was sold to the British Iron and Steel Corporation for breaking-up purposes. This was announced by the company's local agent in Barrow-in-Furness, where the *Viking* was then berthed. Her bell was donated to the town of Fleetwood, with which she had such a long association, and where she was fondly remembered. In 1965, the *Ben-My-Chree* was also consigned to the breaker's yard. On her last voyage to Liverpool there were riotous scenes as the crew broke into stores to access alcohol, and as the ship berthed, the police came on board to restore order. Amazingly in the process of opening cupboards and other hideaways a White Ensign was discovered, clearly a relic of her days in 1944 when she operated in conjunction with the Royal Navy. On the day that she was due to leave Birkenhead to be scrapped, a violent storm blew up confining her to the Morpeth Dock – a final act of defiance in the face of the German tug that was to take her to meet her fate. The following year, officers from the Royal Ulster Rifles visited the Belgian breaker's yard where she lay, in search of some memento of the fact that the ship had embarked the entire 2nd Battalion at Dunkirk. They left with a life ring for their regimental museum.

The same year, the French authorities began work to dismantle the wreck of the *King Orry* outside Dunkirk harbour. The site had been marked since 1946 with two buoys, but being just under the surface it represented a serious hazard to shipping. The works lasted for four months and in the process the hulk was dismantled using both explosives and cutting equipment. This left the wreck a mere one meter above the seabed. No memorabilia is known to survive from the vessel, and it is not inconceivable that anything brass or bronze which might have been salvaged, such as a bell or name plate, would have been sent for scrap.

The *Lady of Mann* was finally scrapped in 1971, though several refits in the 1960s had removed much of her ornate internal woodwork, in order to comply with ever tighter fire regulations for passenger vessels; possibly this was the reason that calls for her to become a floating museum came to naught. Various relics from the *Lady* still survive. One of her lifeboats is still seaworthy, and the triskeles from her stern is today mounted on the exterior wall of the Santon Motel on the Castletown Road. When she left the Mersey for the last time, there were emotional scenes. The inbound *Manxman* acknowledged her with blasts of her siren and the radio message 'Goodbye Old Lady'. Her master, Captain Tom Corteen (who was due to retire himself the following year) told reporters:

> She's still the fastest ship in the fleet and the last example of pre-war Channel steamers. We will never see her likes again.[14]

Another veteran crewman on board was 66-year-old James Cowley, affectionately known by all as 'Snacks', who had joined the company in 1919 and was now the oldest cook in the fleet. When she reached Douglas, 91-year-old Captain Tom Woods was waiting at the harbour to meet her for the last time. He summed up the feelings of many when he said,

> She is the tops. There are none to equal her.[15]

Three days later, the magnificent *Lady of Mann* sailed to Barrow where she was built, to await the ship breakers. In 2010 the wreck of one of the ships lost at Dunkirk, *Mona's Queen* III, was located by French divers, and one of her anchors was raised, with the objective of returning it to the Isle of Man as a memorial. The anchor was unveiled on 29 May 2012, the anniversary of the sinking, and the *Mona's Queen* anchor at Kallow Point now forms the centrepiece of a memorial to all of the Isle of Man Steam Packet Company crewmen who lost their lives at Dunkirk. The people of the Isle of Man can today take justifiable pride in the knowledge that the ships and crewmen, which their small nation placed at the disposal of the Allied cause in 1939, played a not insignificant part in final victory. Indeed, at some crucial moments, such as Dunkirk and D-Day, those ships played a critical role and without them, the outcome might have been very different. It must also sadly be acknowledged that the cost of the part that they played in terms of human life lost was a high one, and as with the Merchant Navy across the board, additionally it must be admitted that this sacrifice has not always been as widely recognised as it might be when these events are commemorated or depicted in mainstream media.

Notes

Chapter One

1. Harry Kinley, Manx National Heritage, Oral History recording SA 0401 (author's transcript)
2. The National Archives, ADM 240/58/59
3. Noel David Glaves James, *Before the Echoes Die Away*, Warwick, 1980, p.84
4. Don Mason, *My War Memoirs 1939-1945*, SL, 2018
5. Harry Kinley, op cit
6. Thomas Cannell, Manx National Heritage, MS10016
7. Harry Kinley, op cit
8. Harry Kinley, op cit

Chapter Two

1. *Isle of Man Examiner*, 7 June 1940
2. Op cit
3. Radcliffe Duggan, Manx National Heritage, MS11490
4. *Isle of Man Examiner*, 7 June 1940
5. G.M.S. Stitt, *H.M.S. Wideawake, Destroyer and Preserver*, London, 1943, p.89
6. G.M.S. Stitt, op cit
7. Radcliffe Duggan, op cit
8. *Isle of Man Examiner*, 7 June 1940
9. *Isle of Man Times*, 7 June 1940

10. www.website.lineone.net/~tom_lee/monas%20isle%20hms.htm
11. Frank and Joan Shaw, *We Remember Dunkirk*, Hinckley, 1990, p.83
12. www.website.lineone.net/~tom_lee/monas%20isle%20hms.htm
13. *Isle of Man Times,* 24 August 1940
14. *Isle of Man Examiner,* 7 June 1940
15. Op cit
16. Op cit
17. Op cit
18. *Belfast Telegraph,* 27 June 1944
19. Robert Addie, typescript narrative, courtesy of Mr Robert Addie (grandson)
20. *Liverpool Echo,* 26 May 1960
21. *Isle of Man Examiner,* 7 June 1940
22. Op cit
23. George Mack, *HMS Intrepid: A Memoir*, London, 1980, p.112
24. *Isle of Man Examiner,* 7 June 1940
25. Op cit
26. Addie, typescript narrative
27. *Isle of Man Times*, 1 June 1946
28. Robert Holmes, manuscript account courtesy of Harry Martland
29. *Isle of Man Examiner,* 10 January 1941
30. Tom Helsby, Manx National Heritage, MS11490
31. Godfrey Hayes, *Starshell*, Vol. 7, No. 43, Summer 2008, pp.16-20
32. Op cit
33. Manx National Heritage, MS09538
34. Op cit

35. Hayes, op cit
36. Hayes, op cit
37. Griff Hughes, Manx National Heritage, MS12624
38. Bill Cheall, *Fighting through from Dunkirk to Hamburg*, Barnsley, 2011, p.xii
39. *Manx Star*, 15 June 1984
40. Bill Lister, account courtesy of Junemary Moyle
41. *Isle of Man Weekly Times*, 20 April 1982
42. Harry Crawley, Manx National Heritage, MS09538
43. *North Wales Weekly News*, 13 June 1940
44. Thomas Cannell, Manx National Heritage, MS10016
45. *Country Life*, 19 February 1981
46. Thomas Cannell, op cit
47. John William Hawkins, Manx National Heritage, Oral History recording SA 0110 (author's transcript)
48. Shaw, *We Remember Dunkirk*, p.125
49. Bernard Bredin, Imperial War Museum Oral History recording #12139 Reel 2 (author's transcript)
50. Tom Corteen, Manx National Heritage, MS09538
51. Manx National Heritage, MS09538
52. Op cit
53. Thomas Cannell, op cit
54. The National Archives, ADM 199/788A, 19 June 1940
55. Op cit
56. Isle of Man Public Record Office, S17/1/1850
57. Manx National Heritage, MS9694/1/15, Minutes of the IOMSPCo Board, 11 January 1941
58. Account courtesy of Audrey Mansell
59. Harry Kinley, op cit
60. *Isle of Man Weekly Times*, 20 April 1982

61. Op cit
62. Harry Kinley, op cit
63. Connery Chappell, *Island Lifeline*, Prescott, 1980, p.116
64. Op cit
65. Michael Davie, *Diaries of Evelyn Waugh*, Toronto, 1976, p.472

Chapter Three

1. *Sunday Sun* (Newcastle), 13 December 1942
2. John William Hawkins, Manx National Heritage, Oral History recording SA 0110 (author's transcript)
3. *Dover Express*, 8 November 1946
4. *Derby Telegraph*, 4 September 1985
5. *Isle of Man Examiner*, 4 December 1942
6. *Liverpool Evening Express*, 4 December 1942
7. *Liverpool Echo*, 4 December 1942

Chapter Four

1. Harry Crawley, Manx National Heritage, MS09538
2. Charles Forte, *Autobiography*, London, 1986, p.44
3. Nikolai Leonida Giovannelli, *Paper Hero*, Douglas, 1971, p.11
4. Dollin Kelly, Manx National Heritage typescript memoir, MS13818
5. F.D. Nickson, Manx National Heritage, MS09819
6. Herbert Eisner, Manx National Heritage, MS11830
7. Edward Winter Anstey, Manx National Heritage, MS12217
8. Laurie Kissack, Manx National Heritage, MS12945
9. *Isle of Man Times*, 31 July 1943
10. *Isle of Man Times*, 1 July 1944
11. *Isle of Man Times*, 23 September 1939

Chapter Five

1. Michael Leslie Melville, *The Story of the Lovat Scouts 1900-1980,* Edinburgh, 1981, p.76
2. *Isle of Man Times,* 28 August 1954
3. Eric Cain, conversation with author
4. Eric Cain, op cit
5. Thomas M Hatfield, *Rudder: From Leader to Legend,* College Station (Texas), 2011, p.113
6. Eric Cain, op cit
7. *Belfast Telegraph,* 27 June 1944
8. *Belfast Telegraph,* op cit
9. Jacques Castonguay, *Le Régiment de la Chaudière,* Levis, Quebec, 1983, p.234
10. *Isle of Man Weekly Times,* 23 March 1982
11. *Manx Independent,* 27 May 1994
12. *Manx Sun,* 15 June 1984
13. *Manx Independent,* 27 May 1994
14. *Isle of Man Weekly Times,* 23 March 1982
15. *Isle of Man Times,* 1 July 1944
16. *Isle of Man Weekly Times,* 23 March 1982
17. *Isle of Man Weekly Times,* 20 April 1982
18. *Isle of Man Weekly Times,* 23 March 1982
19. Op cit
20. *Isle of Man Times,* 1 July 1944
21. *Isle of Man Examiner,* 23 June 1944
22. *Isle of Man Weekly Times,* 23 March 1982
23. https://erenow.net/ww/47-royal-marine-commando-story-1943-1946/5.php
24. https://www.med-dept.com/unit-histories/107th-evacuation-hospital/

25. Brigadier Frank Coutts, *One Blue Bonnet, A Scottish Soldier Looks Back*, Edinburgh, 2008, p.63
26. *Isle of Man Weekly Times*, 23 March 1982

Chapter Six

1. Stan Scott, *Fighting with the Commandos: the recollections of Stan Scott, No. 3 Commando,* Oxford, 2009, p.161
2. *Isle of Man Weekly Times,* 23 March 1982
3. Op cit
4. Op cit
5. Harry Kinley, Manx National Heritage, Oral History recording SA 0401 (author's transcript)
6. Laurie Kissack, Manx National Heritage, MS12945
7. *Mona's Herald,* 12 March 1946
8. Op cit
9. Op cit
10. Op cit
11. Op cit
12. Op cit
13. Op cit
14. *Liverpool Echo,* 16 August 1971
15. Op cit

Bibliography

Castonguay, Jacques, *Le Régiment de la Chaudière*, Levis, Quebec, 1983

Chappell, Connery, *Island Lifeline*, Prescott, 1980

Cheall, Bill, *Fighting through from Dunkirk to Hamburg*, Barnsley, 2011

Coutts, Brigadier Frank, *One Blue Bonnet, A Scottish Soldier Looks Back*, Edinburgh, 2008

Davie, Michael, *Diaries of Evelyn Waugh*, Toronto, 1976

Emanuelli, Hector, *A Sense of Belonging* Lagenfeld, Germany, 2010

Forte, Charles, *Autobiography*, London, 1986

Giovannelli, Nikolai Leonida, *Paper Hero*, Douglas, 1971

Handscombe, David, *King Orry 1913-1940*, Ramsey, 2006

Hatfield, Thomas M., *Rudder: From Leader to Legend*, College Station, (Texas), 2011

James, Noel David Glaves, *Before the echoes die away: the story of a Warwickshire Territorial Gunner Regiment 1892-1969*, Warwick, 1980

Kneale, David, *'Beyond the Limit of Human Endurance': The Stolen Manx History of Dunkirk* in *International Journal of Maritime History*, 2020, Vol. 32 (4)

Mack, George, *HMS Intrepid: A Memoir*, London, 1980

Mason, Don, *My War Memoirs 1939-45*, SL, 2018

Melville, Michael Leslie, *The Story of the Lovat Scouts 1900-1980*, Edinburgh, 1981

Richardson, Matthew, *Isle of Man at War 1939-1945*, Barnsley, 2018
Scott, Stan, *Fighting with the Commandos: the Recollections of Stan Scott, No. 3 Commando*, Oxford, 2009
Shaw, Frank & Shaw, Joan, *We Remember Dunkirk*, Hinckley, 1990
Stitt, G.M.S., *H.M.S. Wideawake, Destroyer and Preserver*, London, 1943

Index

Addie, Robert, 48, 55
Allan, James, 78
Alldridge, John, 9
Almond, H., 183
Ambler, Eric, 47
Anstey, Edward Winter, 140
Ardennes Offensive, 172
Armament, 2, 10–11, 35, 39, 53, 57, 65, 85–6, 89, 93, 153, 157
Armstrong, Charles, 167

Barrow-in-Furness, 75, 114, 120–1, 130–1, 141, 151, 184, 186, 188
Bazeley, Reg, 86
Birkenhead, 21, 34, 119–20, 136, 146, 183, 186
Blair, John Hamilton, 112–13
Boulogne, 30–2, 74
Bradley, Wilf, 81
Bredin, Humphrey, 87
Brest, 99, 106–107
Bridson, Philip 'Ginger', 102–103, 105, 131, 142, 177–8
British Expeditionary Force (BEF) 4, 23, 33, 51
Brown, J.F., 185

Buckingham, Fred, 74
Bushell, W.C., 93

Cain, Dennis, 42
Cain, Eric, 152–3, 155–6
Cain, Tommy, 80
Cain, W.A., 185
Calais, 19, 30, 39, 43, 107, 118, 175
Callow, Lyndhurst, 106, 110
Cannell, Thomas, 16, 82–4, 92
Cannon, Jim, 156
Cheall, Bill, 75–7
Cherbourg, 4, 9, 49, 59, 103, 106, 157
Clague, George, 92
Clewis, Johnny, 176
Clucas, Alex, 19–20
Clucas, Bob, 44–5, 47–8, 51, 54–5, 182
Cobley, Dick, 38
Cooil, J., 183
Corkish, Albert, 78
Corlett, James, 63
Corrin, Fred, 62
Corrin, Jack, 60, 62
Corteen, Tom, 50, 88, 90, 188
Cottage, Frank Thomas, 118–20
Coutts, Frank, 170

Cowell, J., 58
Cowley, James, 188
Cowley, P.B., 88, 95, 98–9
Cowley, Stanley, 67, 74
Craine, Harry, 53
Craine, T.W., 92
Crawley, Harry, 79, 107, 125–6, 130
Crennell, Hugh, 89
Cubbon, J.W., 57, 156
Clyde, River, 16–17, 107, 115, 152

Davidson, A.V., 185
Deal, 12, 78
Divisions,
  44th (Home Counties), 6
  48th (South Midland), 5
Douglas, 21, 26, 42, 49, 55, 58–9, 61–3, 99, 114–15, 131, 133, 135–6, 139–41, 144–7, 151–2, 166, 179–80, 183–4, 186, 188
Dover, 10, 12, 14, 18, 29–30, 36, 39, 41, 44, 54, 56, 61, 70, 74, 92, 98, 174
Doyle, H.A., 185
Duggan, Radcliffe, 24–6, 30–1, 33, 45–8, 55, 155–7, 164
Dunkirk, 12, 22–3, 32, 33–5, 38, 42, 45–8, 50–1, 55–6, 79–80, 82, 84–5, 88–90, 98, 100, 113, 133, 150–1, 161, 187–9

Eason, Reginald, 166
Eisner, Herbert, 137, 139
Elliott, Jeffrey, 2–3, 67, 73

Elton, Jesse, 72
Emanuelli, Hector, 139

Fleetwood, 21, 129, 136–7, 142, 144–5, 186
Folkestone, 84, 98
Forte, Charles, 131–2

Gallagher, J.R., 53–4
Garrett, A.V., 183
Garrett, J.F., 57
Gelling, J.E., 185
Gelling, R.E., 185
Giovannelli, Nikolai, 132
Gloucester, Duke of, 31
Goodwin Sands, 12
Gort, Lord, 4, 33
Granville, Lord, 97–8, 131
Green Howards, 75
Greggor, James, 91
Gribben, Tom, 78
Griffiths, Frank, 182
Guernsey, 103

Halsall, Harry, 176
Hartle, Albert Henry, 118–20
Hassall, Ron, 123
Hawkins, John William, 85, 116
Hayes, Godfrey 'Skinny', 17, 35, 43, 66–8, 70–2
Helsby, Tom, 63–4
Heveron, Jim, 30–1
Hitler, Adolf, 1, 16, 21, 105
Holkham, Archibald 'Jack', 48–9, 51, 110–11, 151
Holman Projector, 86

Holmes, Robert, 58–9, 62, 111
Hughes, Griff, 74
Hughes, Ray, 3

Irish Guards, 30

Jamieson, T.D., 185
Jones, Joseph, 3, 37, 72–3
Jones, R.W.R., 60
Jones, Sam, 3
Joyce, William, 24

Kallow Point, 188
Keig, John J., 166, 168, 185
Kellie, A.A., 185
Kelly, C.H., 183
Kelly, Dollin, 134
Kelly, George Stewart, 147
Kelly, Henry, 113
Kelly, J.E., 120
Kennaugh, George, 130
Kermode, R.R., 63
Kerruish, John, 182, 185
Killey, James, 64
Kinley, Harry, 2, 9–10, 19–21, 35, 99, 100, 104–105, 175
Kissack, Laurie, 142, 177
Kissack, Westby, 63, 185
Kneale, David, 97
Kneale, J., 185
Knowles, Lacey, 50

Lane, Ernest, 66
Lawson, Duggie, 61
Le Havre, 49, 99–103
Lee, James, 74

Lee, Jonathan, 68, 70–1
Leicestershire Regiment, 38
Lister, William, 78, 102, 150, 159–61, 164
Liverpool, 2–3, 62–3, 105, 107, 120–1, 125, 129, 131–6, 147, 150, 152, 166, 186
London, 13–14, 74, 81, 173–4
Lovat Scouts, 149

McCallum, Jimmy, 3
McGinty, E., 120
McLachlan. J., 60
Margate, 59
Mason, C.R., 78
Mason, Don, 6–9
May, A.E., 124
Milford Haven, 108
Mines, 13, 15, 17–18, 21, 25
Merryfield, Louis, 117
Mersey, River, 35, 114, 132–3, 135, 176, 187
Moore, R.B., 130
Morale, 83–4, 86, 88–92, 94, 98
Morgan, Alf, 53
Motion, Roy, 59, 62
Munich Conference, 1
Murphy, F., 185
Mylrea, J., 120

Newcastle-upon-Tyne, 112
Newport, 11
Nickson, F.D., 135
Normandy, 151, 154, 156, 166, 169, 171
Norway, 16

Index   201

Operation Dynamo, 22, 33
Orford, W.O., 127
Osbourne, Gunner, 53
Ostend, 25, 27–8, 169–70, 174–5, 177

Pantin, Charles, 95
Peel, 57, 91, 102, 131, 133, 140, 146–7, 156, 176
Pertwee, Jon, 115
Peters, Frederick Thornton, 122
Pierce, Ted, 81
Poole, 72
Pope, Petty Officer, 41
Port Erin, 117
Port St Mary, 79, 116, 125, 146, 156, 176
Portsmouth, 3, 72, 86, 121
Proudfoot, Frank, 83
Pullan, Edwin, 124

Qualtrough, 91, 95
Qualtrough, Wilfred, 9–10, 19–20
Quirk, J.E., 63–4, 185
Quine, Laurence, 67, 69, 74

Ramsay, Bertram, 22, 24, 33–4, 74, 96–8
Ramsgate, 12, 15, 18, 35
Rangers (US Army), 154–6
Reed, James, 59, 62
Régiment de la Chaudière, 158
Rommel, Erwin, 106–107
Rotterdam, 24
Royal Artillery, 81, 83

Royal Army Service Corps, 38
Royal Army Odinance Corps, 42
Royal Berkshire Regiment, 159
Royal Engineers, 33, 86
Royal Ulster Rifles, 87, 187

Saunders, W., 182
Simpson, Joe, 62
Scarffe, J. Reg, 74
Scott, Stan, 172
Shimmin, Stanley, 77, 160
Ships:
  Arandora Star, 138
  Argus, HMS, 122
  Argo, 123
  Avenger, HMS, 122
  Belfast, HMS, 165
  Ben-my-Chree, 4–6, 8, 11, 16–19, 82, 84–8, 90, 93, 98, 116–18, 149, 152, 155–7, 164, 174–5, 183–4, 186
  British Councillor, 12
  Bruce, HMS, 120
  Bystander, 72
  Caduceus, HMS, 115, 184
  Canterbury, 91
  Chiddingfold, HMS, 150
  Clythness, 72
  Conister, 147
  Courageous, HMS, 12
  Crested Eagle, 58–60, 62–3, 78, 111–12
  Cushag, 146
  Empress of Russia, 121

Evadne, HMS, 135
Excellent HMS, 72
Fenella, 9, 19, 21, 56–8, 60, 63–6, 68, 78–80, 83, 96, 99, 111, 183–4
Grenade, HMS, 65, 68
Intrepid, HMS, 53
Invicta, 175
King Orry III, 2, 10, 12, 14–15, 17, 22, 34, 37, 42–3, 49, 65, 66, 69, 73, 83, 184, 187
King Orry IV, 184, 186
Lady of Mann, x, 4, 11, 19, 75, 77, 87, 103, 108, 139, 149–50, 157–8, 160–1, 163–7, 170, 172–4, 178–81, 183–4, 187–8
Leonardo, 15
Lord Collingwood, 72–3
Lord Grey, 72
Lormont, 14
Malines, 91
Manx Maid, 56, 94, 107, 120, 184
Manxman III, 48–50, 55–6, 87, 95, 98, 106, 114, 116–18, 120, 184, 186
Manxman IV, 187
Mona's Isle, 2, 35–43, 85, 111–14, 130, 184
Mona's Queen III, 4, 9, 19, 23–30, 32, 44, 46, 49–51, 53–5, 79, 91, 130, 183–4, 188
Mona's Queen IV, 184, 186
Patria, 63
Peveril, 146

Prince Leopold, 27
Princess Josephine Charlotte, HMS, 167
Renown HMS, 6
Roberts, HMS, 123
Royal Oak, HMS, 12
Rushen Castle, 1, 115, 129–31, 140–2, 184
St Helier, 92
Samphire, HMS, 123
Scotia, 85–6
Snaefell, 115, 130, 145, 184
Tirpitz, 121
Tynwald IV, 22, 56, 77–9, 81, 87, 90–1, 96, 98, 102–103, 107, 121–7, 133, 150, 183–4
Tynwald V, 186
Valkyrie, HMS, 115
Vanquisher, HMS, 49, 54
Victoria, 1, 129–30, 134–8, 166–7, 169, 175, 177, 184–5
Viking, 21, 56, 80, 99–100, 102, 103, 110, 111, 127, 151, 174, 184, 186
Viking, HMS, 110
Vindicatrix, 152
Warspite, HMS, 165
Windsor, HMS, 42
Witshed, HMS (aka *Wideawake*), 26–9
Wyvern, HMS, 93
Skillicorn, Bobby, 158–9, 161, 163–5, 170–1, 173
Southampton, 4–6, 17, 19, 21, 78, 92, 107

Stitt, G.M.S., 26–7
Studholm, Third Officer, 47
Submarines, 8–9, 12, 113, 122–5, 129, 143

Taggart, J.R., 185
Taylor, Norman, 182
Taylor, Oscar, 107, 186
Teare, A.E., 143, 185
Temple, O.H., 120
Thorp, Denys, 35–6, 39

U-boats, *see Submarines*

Vickers, Tom H., 80, 126

Watterson, Alan, 77
Watterson, C., 185
Watterson, Edgerton, 47
Waugh, Evelyn, 108
Welsh Guards, 30
Whitehaven, 2
Whiting, H., 185
Wodehouse, Philip George, 122
Woods, George, 90, 92, 95
Woods, Tom, 157, 164, 166, 176–9, 181–3, 188